# CU  TO  CUBA

*desk job to dream job*

## HEIDI SIEFKAS

# CUBICLE TO CUBA

*desk job to dream job*

Cover design & interior layout | Yvonne Parks | www.pearcreative.ca

ISBN: 978-0-9971963-2-0 (paperback)
ISBN: 978-0-9971963-3-7 (ebook)
LCCN: 2016918698

# DEDICATION

I dedicate this book to the Cuban people who have welcomed me into their culture and hearts. A sincere *mil gracias* to all who opened the doors into Cuba for me and, in essence, for all of us.

Here's to looking up!

# CONTENTS

# PROLOGUE

Under a banyan tree decorated with white holiday lights, I sipped a mojito and savored a meal of squash, slow-roasted pork, and *moros* (rice and beans). Seated at a table for one on La Ferminia's patio—a place where Fidel himself has dined—I was near Havana ringing in the New Year and a new era. I didn't know that, coincidentally, it was years before, on January 1st, 1959, when Fidel and his revolutionaries turned a page in Cuban history.

I, too, turned a page in my own history. Whether it hinged on a New Year's resolution, the liquid inspiration of multiple mojitos, or a combination of both, I made a big audacious decision that evening. That's when my life as an author and adventurer began.

Join me now! On these pages, I share my adventures of leaving behind the corporate world of "Cubicle Land" to embark on a career of traveling and writing around the world via Cuba. This travelogue highlights another side of Cuba and the perspective gained over my years of life on the road. Be prepared for twists, turns, and even jumps. This adventure starts in Cuba and makes its way to Kauai, Australia, and other far-flung places, but always returning to Cuba for more.

*Cubicle to Cuba* will teach you about Cuba, but it will also inspire you to think out of the cubicle, travel more, and embark on your own Life 2.0.

Make it full of adventure!

# CUBICLE LAND

Life in South Florida was copasetic. I was healthy and loved. I was gainfully employed. My daily commute of fifteen minutes to my Fort Lauderdale office wasn't bad. The job for this start-up company to which I'd lend my marketing and public relations panache even paid well.

However, I felt stuck in Cubicle Land. I wasn't even a worker bee; I was one of the head honchos directing a team of cubicle workers. Although my title was in communications, I dabbled in everything: budgeting, business development, human resources, web design, and coffee-making.

Was status quo what I wanted?

If you've worked for a start-up, you know it's hard work mixed with a grand probability for failure. Depending on the day of the week, the mood of the president, or the attitudes of the investors, the company's course could drastically change at a moment's notice.

I had worked at the start-up only about two months before my New Year's Resolution in Cuba. When I returned to Cubicle Land after driving straight into the office from the Miami Airport, it was one of those days where the investors and VP of Operations had an epiphany. They wanted to do an about-face and scrap our marketing messaging, branding, and direction for sales. Needless to say, I felt like I lived in a Dilbert comic. You know the one. The manager holds a meeting to keep himself busy and then delegates more work for the entire team causing them to head in the wrong direction.

The VP of Operations—whom I and a few others nicknamed Retardiendo because he was Italian and a box of rocks—led this restructuring much like a Dilbert manager would. What kept me sane during the lengthy and subsequent meetings? The daydreams of returning to Cuba and escaping this hell on earth: Cubicle Land.

I didn't know it at the time, but Cuba also has something similar to Dilbert. It's called Lindoro Incapaz, or Lindoro, the incapable. Unlike the typical Dilbert comic Americans see, *Lindoro Incapaz* is a TV show featuring the manager of a government store, Lindoro. A perk of his position is having a government-owned car to be used only for store-related purposes. Of course, Lindoro drives the car and picks up pretty ladies in it. His lack of responsibility leads to imagining a similar lack of the store's success coupled with the antics of employees making peanuts every month. Like in Dilbert, Lindoro isn't a caricature of just one manager but the sum of many. I'm sure you can relate!

Whether it's a Retardiendo or another incapable in charge, to heck with Cubicle Land.

# THE MANNA CALL

While dealing with spreadsheets, editorial calendars, and marketing budgets in Cubicle Land, I received a late-morning call. No, it wasn't from Publishers Clearing House saying I had won millions of dollars. This call involved working in Cuba, which meant I could quit then and there.

The call came from a friend and former colleague. Jacqui and I had worked at the same travel company several years before. She and her husband, Rene, originally from Quebec, lived in Fort Lauderdale. They were sailors, travel lovers, and fun people to hang around with especially when it was wine-thirty.

I answered the phone with "Hey! Long time no see." With a slight French accent, Jacqui said, "I've been watching you and your travels. I have an opportunity for you."

From our conversations as well as on LinkedIn and Facebook, I knew Jacqui worked for another travel agency outside of Florida.

Perhaps she heard of another position through the grapevine for me?

She started, "The last time we had dinner, you said you wanted to work on the other side of travel, with feet on the street leading tours."

"That's right. I'm suffocating in Cubicle Land. What do you have in mind?"

"My agency just got a license to lead educational, people-to-people tours in Cuba. You speak Spanish. You live in South Florida. You've been to Cuba. We start in two weeks with our inaugural trip. It could be your training tour."

The unexpected three-sixty-degree turn of events caused me to stall. I couldn't say a thing. My mind ran the scenario loaded with umpteen questions and uncertain outcomes. Was I ballsy enough to quit my job, knowing the money wasn't the same—but nor was the lifestyle.

After a moment of silence, Jacqui said, "What do you think? Don't you believe you'd be perfect? This is *you*."

"Honestly, I'm blown away. Two weeks is soon. Can I think about it overnight?"

"*Absolutment*! Call me tomorrow."

I hung up the phone and immediately texted my PIC (Partner In Crime), Brian.

*H: would i b stupid to take a job in cuba?*

*B: no go for it! :)*

The remainder of the day, I was the epitome of a Dilbert manager. My mind absent, I got little if anything done. I spent time going to the bathroom, drinking coffee, and rearranging my Post-its®. All I needed was a smoking habit to boot. That would make me the least efficient worker of the day.

That evening at home, I wrote down my thoughts on typical "pros and cons" columns. Seeking advice from my parents wouldn't do, knowing everything *logical* would point to status quo: salary, insurance, and an easy commute to work in the U.S.

However, something was pulling me to the *illogical* route. Yep, my gut!

After a call with Brian, a sleepless night, and a morning spin class, I called Jacqui from my black Honda Accord (aka Honda Limo) on my way to the office. "Jacqui, I'll take your offer to go to Cuba. It's perfect. What do I need to do?"

"Bravo! Most important is doing our paperwork."

"Our paperwork?"

"*Oui, oui.* I'm going with you on the first trip. You get training from our tour manager, Enrique, while I evaluate the hotels and program. Both of you will be sharing the remaining trips of the year."

Jacqui needed to call headquarters, so we hung up without getting all of the logistics. I had some reorganizing to do on my end, and I needed an exit strategy that was more graceful than just quitting. So I quickly put together a plan to have my assistant take my position with a salary increase to mirror more responsibilities. I'd take unpaid leave for a week and a half in

Cuba. Then I'd continue to work for another two weeks to make a smooth transition. I wouldn't leave anyone high or dry. Great!

Before the end of day, I stopped the company's president, Ted, in the conference room. Could I bug him a moment? Most likely, he thought I'd be presenting another campaign or giving him updates on the video production, but nope. I didn't dance around.

I said, "Ted, I was presented with another job I will take, and it's not with a competitor. I'll be leading tours to Cuba with free time to write. I leave for training in two weeks, but after my return, I'd be happy to smooth the transition over to my assistant."

Shocked that anyone would leave a good salary for day wages and tips, he said, "You continue to surprise me, but you're a nomad. Take care of the paperwork with my secretary and your assistant. Sorry to see you go."

That manna call certainly was unexpected, but the benefits would continue to unfold. I didn't realize it then, but Cuba was always there for me.

# A HAIL MARY
# FROM CUBA

My first impression of Cuba? I wanted to know more about this country. The manna call would allow me to transform the sensory overload from that first trip into making sense of it all over the next months (which turned into years).

As on all of my travels, I wrote down my immediate observations and feelings about Cuba in my journal and took hundreds of photos. However, I wanted to share at least *un poco* (a small piece) of it with my clan. As someone who's always glued to her iPhone, I wrote *uno*—yes, only one—Hail Mary email. It came through an archaic PC at Havana's airport.

Subject line: *Hail Mary from Cuba*

Message: *Finally at a place with Internet, I wanted to let you know I have had a wonderful time. My quick snippet/review . . .*

*If you thought last summer in Alaska was different as far as subsistence living and on "Island Time," Alaska is like Manhattan in comparison to Cuba.*

*Without Spanish, this trip wouldn't have been possible.*

*The weather was incredible. I did some hiking, some salsa dancing, lots of eating, some beaching, lots of picture taking, and just gawking at the cars; all the pictures of Havana are spot-on. There are so many 1950s Chevys and Buicks, but here they're pimped out.*

*I certainly learned a lot. It hasn't even sunk in yet.*

*Happy New Year from Habana/Havana!*

*Love you! Heidi*

# MY SPECIAL PERIOD

I think everyone has a point in life when everything goes wrong—just one blow after another. If you read my previous books, you know I'm lucky to even be alive to share this story with you. In 2009 and 2010, I had a special period in which I suffered a freak tree accident that broke my neck. That blow sparked a sequence of other losses including my career, financial security, and most devastating of all—the deterioration of my marriage. I called this my *When All Balls Drop* moment.

Yes, I had lost everything simultaneously: health, marriage, career. However, I turned my losses into a springboard for a life change. I've become a living example of Post-Traumatic Growth. Its opposite effect—Post-Traumatic Stress Disorder—gets all the press, but great things can be created from life's toughest obstacles. Mine was architecting a new life, what I call Life 2.0.

## CUBA'S SPECIAL PERIOD

Unlike *my* Special Period, Cuba's Special Period wasn't a nine-month hardship but a near-decade of economic depression. Because of the dissolution of the Soviet Union and its financial withdrawal from Cuba, the Cuban people suffered grave hardships. *El Período Especial* was marked by rolling power outages of eight hours or more, severe gas and diesel shortages, food rationing, and even famine. Cubans would say there was *nada* special about this Special Period. The era is deeply etched into all who lived it as a time when every Cuban lost twenty pounds and rode a Chinese bicycle. Due to the shortage of oil or electricity, many wouldn't know if they actually acquired something to eat whether they could cook it or not.

However, the upside from Cuba's Special Period (including the worst phase from 1989 to the mid-1990s) came with governmental changes that opened the country to tourism. In turn, tourism brought necessary revenue into the country that continues today. In fact, the idea of *paladares* (private restaurants) and *casa particulares* (B&Bs) started in the 1990s. Cubans could sell delicious guava pastries and even full meals of roasted pork and *malanga* (taro) in their homes. They could rent out rooms to travelers as well. However, at the beginning, all private businesses had to be attached to one's home and employees could only be family members.

In present-day Cuba, private businesses have grown tremendously. Since 2012, President Raul Castro has allowed business owners to operate nail salons, flower shops, and enterprises in many more categories. Today, these private businesses can be housed in separate buildings and run by employees who aren't family members.

For example, on my first trip to Cuba I stayed with a couple, Alexis and Angi, at a *casa particular* in Miramar, a wealthy neighborhood just outside of Havana. They had only one room with a bathroom available. The nightly rent was thirty CUC (Cuban Convertible Pesos—roughly $35) and it included a breakfast with fresh fruit from their backyard as well as bread, cheese, and ham. Over breakfast, Alexis and Angi shared with me their dreams of expanding to three rental rooms, but they had to save a lot and gradually acquire the right materials, as not all supplies or hardware were available. When I left, they gave me their business card to share with other travelers.

Not unlike my gained perspective from my Special Period and Post-Traumatic Growth, the PR spin of Cuba's Special Period foreshadowed what would come from private businesses and tourism in Cuba.

# SLEEPING BENEATH A TREE

No sleeping experience can top my first trip to Cuba.

After touring Havana, I left to get a dose of nature in an area called Las Terrazas, about an hour's drive to the West of the city. With my small-town roots, Las Terrazas and its nature reserve were a needed change of pace from busy, crowded Havana. Nestled in the Sierra del Rosario mountains, this area was at one time deforested but replanted in terraces, thus the name *terrazas*. Rich in lakes, rivers, waterfalls, flora, and fauna, there I could enjoy adventure hiking, swimming in natural pools *(Los Baños del San Juan)*, visiting coffee plantations, and experiencing rural cooking, music, and lifestyle.

It was on my first hike in Las Terrazas that I spotted my first *tocororo*—the national bird of Cuba that's red, white, and blue like the Cuban flag. Even though I've spent more than a hundred and fifty days in Cuba since, I haven't seen another *tocororo*.

This trip was also the first time a Cuban man made a pass at me, but I can't say it was the last time. Cuban men are famous for being *mujeriegos* (womanizers). It just would have been better if the man were not my local guide and driver with whom I had to spend the next two days. Persistent as Roberto was, I left my first trip (and every other trip) to Cuba without a Cuban husband or boyfriend. After my first marriage to a Brazilian, I learned that "Once you go Latin, you do NOT go back."

Although being in nature in Las Terrazas was refreshing, the constant *piropos* (pickup lines) were entertaining but a tad exhausting. So when evening fell, I happily retired to my own room at a *casa particular* (private home). A nearly eighty-year-old man, Margarito, his daughter China, her husband, and their two little girls lived in a small two-bedroom home on a hill overlooking the fertile valley below. This was my first encounter with Cuba's housing shortage. It has been and continues to be common to have multiple generations in the same home and far more people per home that what would be normal in most countries. I didn't know it at the time, but I would be sleeping in the parents' and kids' room. They would house me for a night and sleep elsewhere to make money for the family.

As Margarito showed me my room and bathroom, I stopped in my tracks. Right above my bed running through the bedroom was a large branch of a mango tree. Instead of removing the tree when Margarito expanded his house to accommodate his growing family, he built the room *around* the tree.

Knowing my history with trees, many think I'm afraid of them. Yes, shortly after my accident, I was highly observant of trees and their low-lying branches as well as wind and weather conditions. However, I quickly adapted and put those worries behind me. That evening I had a peaceful sleep—a memorable sleep as well. Still on my bucket list is a desire to sleep in a tree house. It hasn't happened yet, but sleeping beneath a mango tree that's part of a house almost counts, right?

# CHPTR 06

# DOS CURRENCIES

In my travels—whether across Europe (before the Euro) to modern-day travel in South America—I've never needed to understand more than what the exchange rate was for the dollar in the one currency of my locale. I'd exchange U.S. dollars as I needed them; however, I'd prefer to take cash directly out of the ATM or use my credit card. As a seasoned traveler, I'd also have emergency cash squirreled away in my money belt, under my hiking boots' insert, or scattered through my bags. When the shit hits the fan, I knew I'd have to have cash.

Being used to First World banking and technology plus simple math, it was hard to wrap my head around Cuba's two national currencies: the Cuban Peso (CUP) and the Cuban Convertible Peso (CUC). If that seems complicated, just wait. The two types of currencies aren't created equal; they're like comparing apples to oranges.

The CUP is the currency with which citizens are paid from their government jobs. It's also the currency used to purchase staples and domestically produced products. The government instilled the CUC in 1994 during the Special Period to eliminate the use of the U.S. dollar. The CUC is used by tourists for hotels, rental cars, meals, souvenirs, and cigars. It's also used by Cubans to purchase high-ticket items such as refrigerators, washing machines, and imported goods including Spanish olive oils and wines.

The CUC was created to be 1:1 with the U.S. dollar. But over the years I've been traveling to Cuba, the exchange rate has been 1:0.87 or one U.S. dollar to 0.87 CUC. Why? Cuba imposes a ten percent surcharge for converting U.S. dollars plus another three percent surcharge because the transaction involves foreign currency.

There are roughly twenty-five CUPs for every one CUC. For ease, let's say one CUP is approximately a nickel in the U.S. In essence, CUPs are worth peanuts. The mojito that costs anywhere from three to six CUCs in a restaurant or hotel is between seventy-five and one-hundred-fifty CUPs. This doesn't seem like a problem until you know this: the average Cuban (nearly eighty-five percent of the country's population) works for a state school, hospital, manufacturer, hotel, or other business and makes three to five hundred CUPs a month. That's between twelve and twenty CUCs a month. So my high-end mojito at Havana's Nacional Hotel costs anywhere from one third to one half of a Cuban's monthly salary.

How can someone who's employed by the state survive? This is what I ask and so do all of the guests I tour with.

What has happened? Many Cubans have migrated from state employment to private businesses (primarily working with tourists) so they get access to CUCs. Perhaps there are one or two breadwinners in a Cuban multigenerational home. They earn CUCs while the rest of the family earns CUPs and works for peanuts. Without families and neighbors helping each other, most Cubans wouldn't have survived the Special Period, nor would they get by even today.

## MEETING RAIMUNDO

In 2013, Jacqui and I treated ourselves to a convertible car ride in Havana. That's when we met Raimundo. In his early fifties, Raimundo used his father's classic, hot pink, Chevrolet 1957 convertible a couple of nights a week to supplement his daytime state income as a paramedic. His story is quite common. In fact, many Cubans rent classic cars from their owners (including Raimundo's father) to earn extra income. Many of today's Cuban youth are pursuing tourism-related careers as waiters, tour guides, musicians, or something in the arts. Many bypass the free college and postgraduate education in lieu of making money in hospitality immediately. What will happen? It will bring about a "brain drain" in the Cuban society. This contrasts sharply with the success marks of the Revolution: free education, world-renowned healthcare, and high literacy rate.

## ONE CURRENCY ONLY

In late 2013, the Cuban government announced it would revert to one currency only. Which one will it be—the CUC or CUP? I'm no economist, but either would seem difficult. However, Plan A is to have only CUP and eliminate CUC.

Over the years since this announcement, though, both CUP and CUC have been circulating. However, increasingly more of my Cuban contacts prefer U.S. dollars for purchases and tips. Many fear the CUC will disappear and devalue completely. Abroad, the CUC is useless, so people stockpile U.S. dollars in hopes of leaving the country for a brighter future. As of 2017, both CUP and CUC are still in use, with Cuban businesses increasingly accepting U.S. dollars.

Regardless, most Cubans seem to have a built-in calculator "CUP to CUC to *fula*" (Cuban slang for U.S. dollar). They astonish me, like Dustin Hoffman's autistic savant character in the 1988 movie *Rain Man*. But I'm no *Rain Man*. I struggle with numbers. That's why I travel with my iPhone calculator, count my guests twice, and always have a buddy system for my guests, which I call the *compay* system. (See My *Compay* System)

# PACKING LIST
# FOR CUBA

Packing for a trip can be difficult. What's the weather like? What type of activities will you be doing? Will you have laundry available? All these questions would run through my head—and yours, too. However, if you're going to Cuba anytime soon, I suggest packing my top three essentials for traveling there.

## AMERICANS NEED CASH

First, you will need cash if you're an American. If you are from another country, you can disregard this and use your credit and debit cards in Cuba. Mind you, this would be true only at select locations, primarily large hotels, as not all establishments have the phone lines nor infrastructure to process credit or debit cards. Because of more than sixty years of embargo or blockade, American banks don't do business with Cuba and thus you won't find any U.S. banks in Cuba. That reality requires you to bring all the cash you need for expenses, souvenirs, shows, meals, and mojitos.

Back in the States, it has been years since I carried cash except for maybe a twenty in my wallet to cover a rare occasion when a credit or debit card or PayPal isn't accepted. Because most Americans have relied on cards so frequently, budgeting cash isn't their strong suit. More times than I can count, guests confess they've run out of money. Good thing that accommodations and almost every meal are included on the tours I lead. But when you are on a YOLO (You Only Live Once) trip, why skimp on the mojitos or extra souvenirs because you didn't bring enough cash?

How much is enough? It depends on your travel style and if you like art or want to drink wine, beer, or mojitos. However, the quick and dirty is this: *Touring Cuba is not cheap.* You may think this Third World country will be like going to Mexico in the '80s and '90s, but nope. Everything in Cuba is hard to come by and more expensive than you might expect. Why? The U.S. embargo prohibits trade between U.S. and Cuba as well as severely limits the commerce between third-party countries and Cuba. At its beginning in 1962, Cuba had the economic support of the USSR with abundant supplies, including food, medicines, machinery, cars, and more. Since the Soviets pulled out, the economic result of the U.S. embargo can be witnessed in stores. Materials of all sorts from home repair, common foods, and other items are scarce. Contrary to popular opinion, the U.S. embargo cannot be lifted by a president but only by a vote in the U.S. Congress. Thus, until further notice or a vote in the U.S. Congress, Cuba depends on allies that ship goods halfway around the globe. Getting rice from Vietnam or building supplies from China costs money. So getting back to how much money is enough: Gauge at least $100 per person per day in spending money—and that's separate from accommodations and transportation.

Also factor in the ten percent surcharge for U.S. dollars plus three percent for any international currency conversion. As mentioned, one hundred U.S. dollars converts to eighty-seven CUCs. With this unfavorable surcharge rate, many American tourists began traveling with Canadian dollars or Euros. At some point along this multiple-decade dual-currency journey, that has been a favorable solution—until the markets changed. It's a gamble. For example, in early 2016, various guests changed U.S. dollars to Canadian dollars to get a favorable exchange rate. Then the Canadian dollar tanked in value, leaving them short of money they needed. No U.S. credit or debit cards could bail them out.

Cash is still "king" in Cuba. I forecast this to be true for a long time even after the embargo is lifted and/or American banks loosen their restrictions. To use credit cards, of course, phone lines or Internet are needed, which is infrastructure available only in the large cities and hotels. Also, converting into CUCs must be done in Cuba; there are no kiosks in Miami or New York that convert to CUCs.

## CAMPING IN CUBA

Also, be sure to pack toilet paper and hand sanitizer. Yes, going to Cuba is like camping. The women especially will be challenged because, for some reason, the country lacks toilet seats. A trip to Cuba will be like the Suzanne Somers' thigh master routine complete with squatting, hovering, and a good leg workout. You'd find toilet seats, soap, and toilet paper in most hotels, but in standard public bathrooms, an attendant gives you a small amount of paper and probably a heavily used bar of soap you'd prefer to skip.

To prepare for this kind of camping, bring your own hand sanitizer. Hint: a pretty scent covers up times you don't smell fresh after a day of melting in the Cuban heat and humidity.

## PACK YOUR PATIENCE

This is an essential packing item regardless of where you travel, but Cuba in particular. You've heard the expression "island time" when everything runs at a slow, relaxed, no-rush pace. In Cuba, "island time" stretches to another level. So if you're an anal clock watcher, take a deep breath and a chill pill (aka mojito). Simply embrace the slower service and long waits for activities as increasingly more tourists and cruise ships flock to the island of Cuba.

# MY COMPAY SYSTEM

Most authors admit to waiting tables or bartending while writing their novels, but not many can say they took my route of leading tours to Cuba and beyond. It requires being away from home, long eighteen-hour days, and the patience of a saint, but my "office" always changes.

When on tour, my number one goal is to bring everyone back from a fun-filled adventure healthy and happy. However, on my training tour, I made a big boo-boo. In the midst of a small accident where an elderly woman stumbled out of the tub and sprained her finger, my mentor, Enrique, went to the international clinic with the guest. In the meantime, I was to escort the group to the local botanical garden and back. I counted the group with what I thought was the amended number of correct guests. Then, we left. Ten minutes down the road, our local guide, Yislaine (who later became my good friend and work partner for a year) received a call saying a female guest was left behind. I felt stupid. After a slight change, in a rush, and due to little sleep, I had counted *wrong*. I failed. If I'm to bring everyone back to the U.S., I need to at least count everybody *right*.

Knowing this was a simple thing that could interrupt my most basic duties—to not leave anyone behind—I needed a solution. So I piggybacked on the buddy system used in the military, in SCUBA diving, and even in kindergarten. However, this idea needed a Cuban flair.

Most people know that *amigo* is friend in Spanish, but saying "*amigo* system" was far too boring. I chose *compay* (COM-pie), which is primarily used in Cuba to mean friend or *compadre* (similar to comrade in Russian). Perhaps you've heard of Compay Segundo, a famous musician from the Buena Vista Social Club. So on my second tour and every tour after, I explained the word *compay* and picked a *compay* for each traveler. The requisites were that: 1) No two *compays* could be roommates and 2) It was better if they didn't know one another. This provides more security and certainty that all guests received the asked-for wake-up calls or that the night owls came back from the disco. It also sparks getting to know more people on the tour, which is a big benefit of the whole experience.

Although many thought this system childish at first, they realized it made every stop or meeting point more efficient. If a *compay* went missing, instead of going down the list name by name, I'd know exactly who to look for in the market, square, or theatre. Although it started out as a CYA (Cover Your Ass) for me, the *compay* system morphed into appreciated group bonding. By being accountable for another person for eight days or more, friendships were sparked and lots of photos with *compays* resulted, too.

The *compay* system works. Albeit at times, some guests I'd like to lose.

# PEEPEE COIN— SOCIALISM IN CUBA DOESN'T COVER TOILETS!

Regardless of your politics—red, blue, indie, or other—I learned that socialism (whether in Cuba or elsewhere) has its benefits. For example, everyone gets free education and healthcare. However, the buck stops (at least in Cuba) at the *baño*.

In Cuba, bathroom quality is questionable at best. As mentioned earlier, it's wise to bring your own toilet paper and hand sanitizer. Don't be shocked, ladies, when you see that somewhere along the line, toilet seats are gone. Most of the toilets, except in the hotels and nicer *paladares*, don't have them. Think about it. At Home Depot, which doesn't exist in Cuba, when you buy a commode, you have to buy a toilet seat separately. In places where home repair goods are in limited supply, toilet seats don't make the cut!

With all of the minuses of the *baños*, it's hard to believe that in a country with free education and healthcare, you pay a twenty-five *centavos* fee to use the *baño*. Yes, you must pay to use the restroom. At most *baños* across Cuba stands an attendant with a small table and a basket outside the lavatory stalls. This person, male or female, offers you entrance to the restroom along with one or two squares of Cuban toilet paper in exchange for a twenty-five *centavos* coin. If you want more squares, you bring your own TP packs. You can also employ the technique used by *Seinfeld* character Elaine and ask for a square from a *compay*, but sometimes a person can't spare a square!

Keep in mind that every *baño* is different except for needing twenty-five *centavos*, which I renamed the peepee coin circa 2013. Some have liquid hand soap and others an antique bar of soap. Some are hooked up to running water, others not. If there's no running water, the attendant follows with a bucket to fill the tank and flush down your peepee and/or doodoo.

Remember, don't throw your paper in the toilet. Place all tissues as well as sanitary napkins, tampons, or other items in the wastebasket next to the commode. The plumbing is weak on its best days, so do yourself (and the next person) a favor by using the trash can.

I've never been fond of paying for a bathroom attendant, but let's face it, when you really have to go—whether it's traveler's diarrhea or one beer in, one beer out—you'd gladly pay more than twenty-five *centavos* to go.

27

# SAVE WATER, DRINK RUM, AND SHOWER WITH A FRIEND

No doubt you've seen a T-shirt from Mexico that says "Save Water, Drink Cerveza" to promote Corona beer drinking as well as bring humor to those who get Montezuma's revenge. Through traveling to Cuba, I have taken that message to a whole new level.

"Save Water, Drink Rum, and Shower with a Friend" defines my way to let people know the water is unsafe to drink and in extreme shortage, even at the hotels where we stay. On several occasions, I've had unexpected water issues.

After the water crisis in Flint, Michigan, began in 2014, I found myself in Cienfuegos, a beautiful city of one hundred-fifty-thousand people on the south-central coast of Cuba. The first morning after our late-night arrival at the hotel, I noticed that the water coming out of the tap ranged in color from yellow to brown. I immediately reported it to the reception and maintenance people. (Confession: I had noticed a little discoloration as I showered that morning after my run, but I didn't want to skip a shower because of yellow, brown, or cold water. Growing up on a Wisconsin farm with its own well and cistern, I was used to this.)

The hotel people explained they'd recently received a water truck delivery, as they weren't connected to city water. Perhaps the water tank on the roof had rust in it that got stirred up with the delivery. While some guests showered, others opted to wait it out. As an apologetic gesture, the hotel manager gave all the guests extra bottles of water for drinking and brushing their teeth. Management predicted that, after running the water for the remainder of the day, it would clear up. Indeed, by day two, it finally cleared up—another example of patience and island time.

## NOT EVEN A DROP

After one of my morning runs along the Cienfuegos seawall, dripping in sweat, I entered my room, peeled off my drenched spandex, and finagled my way out of my sports bra. There I stood before the shower, naked and smelly. I turned the two knobs and—nothing. Only a slight sound of pipes creaking. Unbelievable. I turned them again off and on, off and on. Still nothing, *nada*, not even a drop of water.

Faced with a half-hour before breakfast, I reviewed my options: skip the shower, use bottles of water from the mini-bar, or turn to my disposable facecloths for removing make-up. I opted for the last one, a somewhat French bath with bug repellent and sunscreen as my perfume. Then I quickly went down to the lobby to report the issue and find a solution for my guests who would shortly discover the same thing—only two bottles of water for each guest to brush teeth, wash face, and flush toilet. Thankfully after a full day of touring, we returned to the hotel not only to have running water but *hot* water that wasn't yellow. Victory!

A good rule of thumb: save water, drink rum, AND shower with a friend.

More on rum to come.

**CUBA | CHPTR 11**

# WHEN LIFE GIVES YOU LEMONS, MAKE CANCHÁNCHARAS

You've heard it time and time again whether from your mother, your friends, or a pop culture TV host: When life gives you lemons, make lemonade.

It's healthy to live in a manner of spinning negatives into positives. Like you, I've been dealt both good and bad hands of cards. It comes down to what you do with any situation that makes the difference.

After nearly twenty trips to Cuba, I have witnessed the spirit of the entire island as turning lemons into lemonade. It's a Cuban way of life. The Cubans I've met are passionate and kind with a stoic essence of the Midwest or Scandinavia. However, it's their zest

31

for life and living in the moment that makes Cuban culture rich and distinct. If life deals them a bad hand of dominos or worse, they move on, perhaps laughing about it. They enjoy the simple things in life such as smoking a good Cuban cigar, drinking a Cuban coffee, sipping Havana Club Reserve, or just watching the world go by with a friend, neighbor, or family member.

I thought that this play on words—combined with a Cuban cocktail recipe for a *canchánchara*—would be a way to make the lesson sink in. Who doesn't like a good cocktail now and again? A *canchánchara*, the signature drink of Trinidad, Cuba, is easy to make and turns those bitter lemons into a sweet libation.

So, make no excuses for ignoring your duty and your health. When life gives you lemons, make *cancháncharas!*

## CANCHÁNCHARA RECIPE

Ingredients:

- 2 oz. Cuban rum *(ron cubano)* or *aguardiente*
- 1 tbsp. honey *(miel)*
- 1 tbsp. lime juice *(limón)*
- 1½ oz. soda water *(agua gaseaada)*
- Ice *(hielo)*
- Ceramic cup or lowball glass *(taza o vaso)*
- Straw or stirring stick *(absorbente o palito)*

Instructions:

1. Pour honey and rum into your desired cup or glass.
2. Stir with a straw or stirring stick until the honey dissolves.
3. Add lime juice, sparkling water, and ice.
4. Serve with a toast. *Salud!*

Most think that a *canchánchara* is easy to make but difficult to pronounce. I can attest it is rather *fácil* to make AND, after one *canchánchara,* pronouncing it gets easier. Don't believe me? Try it! Can-CHAN-cha-ra with the stress on the second syllable.

# POR FAVOR
# VLADIMIRO

From the 1960s through the 1990s, it seemed Russia and Cuba were BFFs (Best Friends Forever). Okay, maybe that's not the best way to describe being economic and military allies during the Cold War. However, these two countries banded together against the superpower to Cuba's north, but I swear this label has significance.

Just like BFFs, Cuba's Castro and USSR's Khrushchev did ballsy things such as bringing a Russian nuclear missile to Cuba, which put the entire world on edge during the 1962 Cuban Missile Crisis. However, at the same time, like BFFs, they supported one another. Russia floated Cuba economically for three decades, supplying its ally with subsidized products.

How does one honor a friendship of such worth? By giving Russian names to a generation of Cubans. I have met many Cuban men and women with the names Conrado, Boris, Vladimiro, Olga, and Katia. After expecting Latin names such as Carlos, Victor, or Christina, hearing Russian names threw me for a loop—or better said, a time warp.

## ROLLING MUSEUM

Russia's power and role in Cuba has not only shown up in the names of a generation but also as part of its rolling museum. People automatically think about Cuba and its 1950s American cars: Chevy Bel Aire, Cadillacs, Pontiacs, and Buicks. However, another wave of cars has made a splash on the Cuban roads: Russian Ladas and Mosoviches. These utilitarian four-door sedans that look like boxes on wheels are similar to some of the Russian architecture of the 1970s and '80s. Ladas and Mosoviches were on the roads but during the severe gasoline shortage of the '90s were seen sparingly as were all cars. That's when China, another BFF, supplied Cuba with millions of bicycles.

Today, Ladas and Mosoviches are still on the roads as private cars and even taxis. They don't have the "wow" factor of the spectacular American cars, but not every car in Cuba is what it seems. Many of these American classics look authentic on the exterior, but the interior could be held together by Lada parts, Chinese components, or even a Cuban version of duct tape.

## RUSSIAN CONNECTION

At this book's writing, English was Cuba's primary foreign language taught in school. But commonly, the parents of Russian-named children studied Russian, traveled to Russia, or even graduated from university as Russian literature scholars. The old adage "you are the company you keep" rings true with Cuba and Russia. Another mojito, *por favor* Vladimiro, and *nostrovia* (meaning *salud* or cheers).

# INCOMUNICADO

Just like going out into the deep woods of Alaska, much of my time in Cuba was *incomunicado* (unreachable), the Spanish word for being deprived of any communication with others. Although Cuba is only ninety miles from Key West, it has little to no Wi-Fi. Plus, international calls and texts when possible are expensive! Yikes! This tested my addiction to my iPhone as well as my recall of information. I didn't realize how much I relied on Googling something until I traveled to Cuba.

It's hard to fathom, but life does exist without the Internet. By removing the constant clutter of apps, emails, and social media, my belief in the mantra Look Up was strengthened. These two powerful words remind people to be in the moment and spin each situation positively. Likewise, being *incomunicado* forced me to appreciate the NOW. What a blessing.

## STATUS OF THE INTERNET

The majority of my time in Cuba was spent leading educational tours for groups of Americans. All of these visitors had cell phones, and many said they welcomed getting away from their digital life awhile. However, there was always someone in the group who experienced phone and Internet withdrawal symptoms: anxiety, difficulty concentrating, even headaches. Fortunately, some of our Cuban hotels have been making the Internet available for guests *poco a poco* (little by little).

During my first two years in Cuba, the government-run telecommunications company ETESCA would have Internet cards for sale at the reception in the large government-run hotels. With these cards, guests would receive a login and password to use the sole archaic PC in the lobby and by the minute. (Most hotels didn't have business centers and often there was only one PC for a hotel with hundreds of guests. Internet was available with the cards, but only from this one landline computer. It reminded me of buying gas in Florida after a hurricane.)

The reverse also occurred. Sometimes the PC was available but the reception had run out of cards. It's another example of the cart before the horse or, in Cuba, *empezar la casa por el tejado* (starting the house with the roof). To contact the States in emergencies, it had to happen through landline calls from the reception of the hotel. Even from the Nacional Hotel in Havana, we made operator-assisted phone calls costing more than two bucks a minute. Thankfully, most members of the support team in Cuba—from local guide to driver—had cell phones. These were essential. Each trip, I would buy phone cards to charge *(recarga)* their phones as a way to assist in coordinating services.

In late 2014, I saw my first Facebook post from Havana by Enrique, the tour manager who had trained me. I gasped and immediately commented, "OMG, you can actually update from Havana. I can't wait!" And when I returned twice in 2015, I was able to purchase an Internet card for ten bucks so I could have slow Wi-Fi in the large hotels. However, it was only good when I was in the hotel, which was really only for sleeping. The typical, eighteen-hour day of touring through Cuba didn't allow for much more than another Hail Mary email back to headquarters in the States and to my clan. I'd spend most of my time finding the weather report for the following day. How hot? Any rain? Is there a hurricane in the Caribbean?

My inaugural Facebook post was a reply to the question "Did you see the Super Bowl in Cuba?" I answered the February 3, 2015, post this way:

*The verdict . . . Yes, we saw the Super Bowl in Cienfuegos, Cuba. Right from the hotel bar, we sipped mojitos, not Budweiser.*

# CHPTR 14

# EVERYTHING AND THE KITCHEN SINK

As a child, my mother instilled in me to always bring a little something if invited over to someone's house for dinner, a party, or a sleepover. By practicing what she preached, word of her phenomenal baking talent got around. From apple pies and cream-cheese-frosted carrot cake to tiramisu and holiday cookie trays that would make Martha Stewart bow, my mom knows her way around the kitchen.

In my own way, I took this lesson into my travels. Whether on personal travels or touring trips, I always have a stash of gifts. Regardless of the country, I have a handful of name-brand hats, T-shirts, stickers, makeup, toiletries, clothes, magazines, and candies. While preparing for my next trip to Cuba, I'd send out messages to my friends to raid their closets of hot ticket items:

baseball hats, sports T-shirts, baby clothes, and toiletries of all types. Then I gave these items to people who made a difference in my travels—whether they were local guides, drivers, or hotel staff. The bonus? Many of them have become good friends.

Coincidentally, these gifts opened a door to another role—that of a mule. No, not becoming a cross between a horse and a donkey but bringing items from the States to my Cuban friends. Imagine the countless items they couldn't find in Cuba because of the embargo or the cost. My flights to Cuba limited me to forty-four pounds per bag, but from the look of all the other Cuban and Cuban-American passengers with oversized bags and boxes at check-in, you wouldn't think a limit existed! With no Menard's, Ace Hardware, or Home Depot in Cuba, it was common to see airport carts full of plumbing, TV screens, IKEA furniture, bicycle tires, and large shrink-wrapped, oversized boxes and bags. One time I even saw a kitchen sink roll by! Traveling more incognito than other passengers bringing *pacotillas* (gifts or little packages from abroad), I always fit my items into my one large worn-and-torn suitcase nicknamed "behemoth."

## SOUGHT-AFTER ITEMS

In the beginning, I brought in requested items from a written list drawn up during the previous month's trip. Highly sought-after things on my first trips were toothpaste, mouthwash, dental floss, deodorant, men's razors, and children's vitamins. Apparently, for both toothpaste and deodorant, people dealt with countrywide shortages. Surprisingly, requested items were also adult diapers. With Cuba's aging population, they were needed yet expensive for those on a pension. Pensions are sixty percent of their Cuban Peso (CUP) salaries. Sixty percent of peanuts is living on crumbs.

41

It's not unlike many American retirees, except that Cuban retirees don't have the added costs of expensive medications and other healthcare needs.

When my friends' immediate necessities were met, I addressed the next wave of "muling" items. In my second round of *pacotillas*, I brought in perfume from Victoria's Secret, facial hair bleach, shoes, and large-memory flash drives to store photos, music, and downloaded movies.

## REVERSE MULING

You may think I only "muled" items from the U.S. to Cuba, but in one particular case, I did the reverse as a medical favor for a Cuban-American friend, Otumara. Her family had moved to the States in 1969, but she still had an extended family in Havana as well as Holguín, a province in the Northeast of the island. Through phone calls, she learned that Cuba was making a serum for a skin discoloration called vitiligo that her son, Rafael, had. Although effective, the serum wasn't available in the States because it was made from human placentas.

Through communications with a professional friend in Havana, we located the serum, and Otumara sent cash with me to pay for it. I arrived in the States "muling" in reverse medical supplies for a Cuban-American. What irony!

## A COMMUNICATIONS EVOLUTION

My "muling" went through an evolution. It started in the way the lists were communicated. First, they were handwritten but by the end of the first year, I received email messages. Because few Cubans had access to Internet service, someone who had it through a government job would send me an updated list on behalf of a friend. The communications from old school to email mirrored Cuba's progress over the years.

After nearly a year of absence from Cuba while living in Kauai in 2014, I returned in early 2015 after Presidents Barack Obama and Raul Castro announced more open relations between Cuba and the U.S. Although I had a hunch all the hubbub was smoke and mirrors, I let the "muling" list dictate my judgment on change. Yes, diplomatic relations had been rekindled but hadn't touched the lives of the average Cuban. My evidence was that the "muling" items stayed the same; my friends still asked for basic toiletries including laundry detergent.

## HOTSPOTS

In 2016, my "muling" lists changed dramatically when Cuba created Wi-Fi hotspots in Havana, Santa Clara, Cienfuegos, and other major cities. Previously, the Internet was only for those needing it for their government jobs. However, even those privy to the Internet had limited access, minutes, and small bandwidth. With these hotspots, more Cubans could access the Internet with a smartphone or tablet by purchasing two CUC cards from ETESCA, the government communications company.

Still, Internet access is cost prohibitive for most Cubans. When you make between three hundred and five hundred CUPs a month at a government job, two CUCs is more than ten percent of your wage. Plus, you need to buy a device such as a cell phone or tablet.

With my behemoth, little by little I brought in unlocked cell phones and tablets. The hunger for information and connection was highly evident. That's why I became the Cuban equivalent of a mini Best Buy.

## DOORS OPEN TO THE WORLD FOR CUBANS

In a culture that values family, the Internet provides a way for families living in separate countries to communicate weekly or even daily. On one of my trips to Havana, I witnessed a family of four sitting in a small car parked on 23rd Street (La Rampa—one of the hotspots as well as a meeting point for most *Habaneros* at night). The parents sat in the front seats accessing the Internet using an app called IMO (similar to Facetime) to talk with relatives. Meanwhile, the kids in the backseat shared a tablet and played a game. In such a well-read and educated society, the Internet continues to open doors to the world. What a delight to be a part of this progress and help my Cuban friends communicate and learn.

I come from a family of teachers. Both of my grandmothers who were born in the early 1900s were college educated and became primary school teachers. My parents, too, were both lifelong educators. In essence, teaching and sharing information are part of my DNA, and the teacher in me felt proud.

Although being a "mule" may not appear like teaching, gifting others access to knowledge certainly is! Once a teacher always a teacher.

# MY SISTER FROM ANOTHER MISTER—YISLAINE

I first met Yislaine, a dark, beautiful mid-twenty-year-old from Santiago on my training trip to Cuba with Jacqui and Enrique. She and I found ourselves in the same boat. Yislaine was new to touring with Americans but had led groups of Canadians and French. She spoke French, English, and Spanish fluently.

Her name was not unlike thousands of others born in the '80s in Cuba starting with Y, but it certainly was a hard name for the guests to pronounce (Is-LANE-ee). Similarly, I was brand spanking new to touring with groups through Cuba. I only had English and Spanish with a noticeable Castilian accent. My name was easy for my American guests but not so on the Cuban side. To make my name more Cuban, I adopted Heyde (pronounced HAY-dee like the country Haiti with a D).

After landing at Cienfuegos airport, Yislaine greeted the tour group wearing her blue company T-shirt and miniskirt. With a long, dark ponytail, bold brown eyes, and a smile, Yislaine fit the bill of all the visions of beautiful Cuban women. She introduced herself to Enrique and kissed him on the cheek. Despite his being a veteran tour manager throughout Cuba, she'd never worked with Enrique before. Yislaine hid her beginner's nerves well.

At dinner that first evening when Enrique introduced both Jacqui and me, everything clicked. Jacqui and Yislaine spoke in French while Enrique and I talked through details with the driver in Spanish and prepared for the following day's trip to Trinidad.

After spending a week with Yislaine, I knew that, as a team, we could do an excellent job. Enrique, with his discerning taste, preferred to work with another guide. Learning that, I requested working with Yislaine on all my tours. As a result, in that first year Yislaine and I spent more than eighty days together, which was more time than I spent with Brian, my boyfriend and PIC (Partner In Crime), or family members. As she shared her culture with me and I mine, Yislaine became my "sister from another mister."

All of my takeaways from Cuba I owe to my Cuban friends. However, my greatest teacher was Yislaine. After our first mistake together when we'd left a guest at the hotel, she knew I felt like a failure. She felt the same. So to smooth things over, Yislaine told me, "In Cuba, there are no problems, only situations. One situation, one mojito. Two situations, two mojitos." I turned, laughed, and hugged her.

## ONE SITUATION, ONE MOJITO

Over the course of the next several trips together, we encountered many situations that could have been perceived as problems: a mandatory bus stop by the police for fumigation, numerous trips to the international clinic, and inevitable hotel hiccups. After resolving what we could in each, we looked at each other with smiles, saying in our heads "one situation, one mojito."

We'd become so close, I knew when Yislaine wasn't feeling well or what story she'd tell next. She automatically knew what I would order at a particular restaurant and if I'd a bad night sleep the night before.

Although I couldn't introduce her to my PIC who was in the States, I met Yislaine's other half, Javier, at a *paladar* (privately owned restaurant) on the Malecón in Havana. Over a few Cristal beers, she and Javier retold their history. They had been sweethearts from the same hometown in the Eastern province of Santiago. Javier had worked with livestock and with Yislaine's father. She moved to Havana for her university studies, sharing an apartment on the outskirts with her aunt, uncle, and sister. Afterward, she was assigned her mandatory social service as payback to the Cuban government for her free education. She worked as a French translator in a public relations firm, which led to guiding tours for French Canadians and subsequently working with this tour company. Javier had moved in with Yislaine's family and found employment at the local milk production plant.

I asked them, "Do you plan on getting a place of your own?" Yislaine and Javier both shook their heads. With housing at a shortage, they knew getting a place of their own was out of their reach financially. For young Cuban couples, it was common to live with either parents or the family of your significant other. It wasn't a matter of which parents you got along with best or wanted you but which family had the most room!

## DINNER AND GIFTS

That evening, I did what my mother had taught me to do—I brought a gift to a special dinner. I gave Javier a Red Sox T-shirt. When he took the shirt, I saw he absolutely loved it. His eyes grew wide as well as his smile. Then he went to the bathroom and came back wearing the Red Sox shirt. Yislaine later told me he wore the shirt to work the following day, and she commented, "Javier thinks you are *pan de gloria*—you know, the glorious sweet rolls. It's a compliment!"

To surprise Yislaine on that same trip, I had brought a gift from one of Jacqui's recent trips to Nevada—a glitter shirt from Las Vegas. Yislaine didn't run to the bathroom to change; she immediately put it on over her blue work shirt, and then she hugged me.

Yislaine and I didn't go around the world in eighty days that year, but we survived the onslaught under intense pressure: more than one hundred and fifty guests, countless bouts of diarrhea, allergic reactions, doctor visits, excessive heat, sleepless nights, and severely inebriated guests. After "herding cats" with someone for that long, Yislaine and I will always be sisters from another mister.

## MOJITO YOUR SITUATIONS AWAY

After sharing the wisdom of mojitos, I wanted to give you a way to turn your problems or situations into a thing of the past with a true Cuban mojito recipe.

Remember one situation, one mojito; two situations, two mojitos; three situations, three mojitos. When all your balls drop with a full-blown catastrophe, make four—but be prepared to hit the floor.

## MOJITO RECIPE FOR 4

Ingredients:

- 6 oz. light rum *(ron)*
- 6 tbsp. lime juice *(jugo de limón)*
- 4 tbsp. sugar *(azúcar)*
- Club soda *(agua gaseada)*
- Bitters *(angostura)*
- 12 mint sprigs *(hierba buena)*
- 4 slices of lime *(limón)*
- Highball glass *(vaso)*

Instructions:

1. Place all ingredients in shaker minus limes, 4 sprigs of mint, bitters, soda water.
2. Pour shaken mixture into 4 glasses of ice.
3. Splash each glass with soda water to taste.
4. Add one to two drops of bitters to each glass.
5. Garnish with one fresh sprig of mint and a lime slice.

Enjoy the mojito recipe. It's cheaper than therapy!

# MAGIC LITTLE BLUE PILL

A hazard of traveling is catching a bug from something you eat, drink, or touch. You never really know where you got it. You can speculate, but you definitely know it when you have it. Nothing puts you more "in the moment" than traveler's diarrhea.

Take a moment. When was the last time you had the runs? You didn't have minutes or even seconds to spare to find that bathroom, right? For the span of your episode of Montezuma's Revenge, you put yourself on high alert for any and all *baños*.

You may think the only magic little blue pill is Viagra, but I beg to differ. I trust the magic of another little blue pill called Imodium. In fact, I carry at least two bottles of these magic stop-you-uppers with me for every trip. "Take two now and another one four hours later and call me in the morning."

## CLOSE CALLS

Because I've traveled to Cuba so frequently, I should have resident status, but I still get what I call the *chorros de Cuba* (Cuban squirts). On numerous occasions, whether traveling with groups or solo, I've faced countless close calls. There are two epic *chorros de Cuba* I share: one of my own and the other demonstrating why I always carry a sarong.

In a *paladar* in the Vedado neighborhood of Havana, I sat at the dinner table with a dozen of my guests when I began to feel my tummy churn. I could barely drink my sparkling water or stomach my fried plantain chips. Trying to distract my sensations, I continued to share my stories of previous trips to Cuba and learn about the people at my table. However, I knew the moment had arrived when the impending disaster pains came along with increased salivation.

I excused myself quickly and went into the tiny women's restroom, closed the door, and debated which end needed the toilet first. There was no toilet seat and a wire wastebasket with no liner in the corner. Under normal U.S. situations, I would have sat on the toilet seat and grabbed a basket to puke. This time, I had to improvise. So I whipped up my skirt and hovered over the toilet no sooner than the fire hoses of my angry belly let loose. Immediately, I flushed the toilet because round two was imminent but from the other end. If my first batch didn't go down quickly, I would have to barf in my Cuban hat, I thought.

Hunching down to the floor smelling of urine, I threw my hat behind me and heaved, releasing whatever remained in my stomach and trying not to cause an encore from my rearend.

Luckily, there was toilet paper to wipe my mouth and watering eyes. Feeling less than a million bucks but much better than before, I stood up, arranged my clothing, grabbed my hat, and used my hand sanitizer. Straight to the bar I went to ask for a sparkling water with bitters. I needed something to keep the queasiness at bay and wash down two of my magic little blue pills.

## CHORROS DE CUBA

The other unforgettable *chorros de Cuba* experience happened in Old Havana. While touring its cobblestone streets and principal squares, one of my guests, who had already gone to the clinic earlier in the trip, was put "in the moment" by a case of *chorros de Cuba*. Luckily, both Yislaine and I knew the best hotel to sneak into quickly. She made it to the bathroom in time but didn't get all of the *chorros* into the *baño*. Needless to say, no one likes a dirty diaper or a poopy pair of pants.

After quickly assessing the situation, Yislaine discreetly escorted our guest to a nearby taxi to take her and her husband to the hotel, while I joined the rest of the group in the Old Square. I learned that I needed a Band-Aid for times this might occur again. Not always will there be a bathroom and transportation close by. So I always bring along a sarong. It can be used as a towel, a picnic blanket, or an impromptu skirt or kilt for when anyone poops their pants. With a sarong, you can never go wrong!

# HEADLAMP IN HAVANA

In the middle of the night in a Miramar hotel outside of Havana, I answered a knock on my door to find a male employee holding a flashlight. I recognized him from seeing him in the lobby. I tried to switch on the lights but to no avail. Power outage. He quickly said one of my guests needed me. I hoped she wasn't hurt.

After clumsily putting on my sneakers, I proceeded to my backpack and grabbed my camping headlamp from it. I often used it on my early morning runs so I could see and avoid tripping over the cracks in the pavement and sidewalk before the sun came up.

After speaking to the hotel worker on the walk to my guest's room, I knew exactly who had called complaining of the power being out—Mary. She was hard to please unless it somehow dealt with booze. Also, she was easily frazzled unless already self-medicated. In fact, earlier in the trip, she missed a day because she had pulled an all-night bender. In privacy the evening after, I said to her, "Mary, I'm a little concerned about you. You are drinking quite a bit." Well, that wasn't what she wanted to hear (nor does anyone who has a substance abuse problem). She replied defiantly, "I'm on vacation. I can do what I want. I haven't done anything wrong." I responded, "Yes, you are on vacation. I'm just concerned. Your whereabouts in Cuba, your safety, and your health are my responsibility."

That night when I arrived at Mary's room, a maintenance man was waiting outside. After knocking, both men and I entered the room. Mary was already in a tizzy that she couldn't see anything. Concerned that the two employees didn't understand her complaint, she demanded I translate. That puzzled me. I knew they understood because they had brought a flashlight for her. Power outages are problems; however, shouldn't she have been sleeping? At that hour, most people would never have known. They'd sleep right through it.

To reassure her that the hotel and maintenance people were aware of the outage, I said, "Thank you for helping. Other than using a flashlight, all we can do is wait. Hopefully within an hour, the power will come back on."

Still, she was clearly upset. "But the air conditioning!" So I walked to the windows and cracked open all three of them, then said, "Outages are not typical. This most likely will be short. It isn't like the 1990s during the Special Period when the power outages lasted eight hours at a time." With that, she appeared subdued enough for all of us to leave. I wished her a good night: "*Que duermas con los angelitos.*" ("Sleep with angels" or "sleep tight.")

Within an hour, the electricity came on—about the time my alarm would go off. So much for *my* sleep with angels. The upside was I already had my headlamp ready for my early morning run.

## THE BEST WAY TO SEE A CITY—RUNNING IN HAVANA

You get the view of a place differently by getting around on foot—something I wrote in *With New Eyes* about Buenos Aires. That's how I've found my way in new cities, including Havana. I have run each morning, witnessing the city awaken with bread being delivered, kids bicycling to school, and water delivery trucks (*pipas*) making their rounds.

On one particular morning, I was running on the Malecón where a few men were fishing, but no one else was running. A third of the way through my roughly five-kilometer run, a tall slender man passed me on foot. I continued to follow him, albeit a block behind him. Before long, he looked back while continuing to run and then looked back again. Suddenly he yelled, "*Venga*," which means "Come on." He was encouraging me to put in more effort, so I sped up and started running with him.

"*Yo soy Reynaldo. Y tú ?*" (I'm Reynaldo. And you?)

Between breaths, I answered, "*Yo soy Heidi. Soy de los Estados Unidos. Vivo en la Florida.*" (I'm Heidi. I'm from the States. I live in Florida.)

Without being winded at all, Reynaldo commented it was nice to see a woman running. Not many people run in Havana, let alone women, he said. I explained that I run because I *can*. Little by little, I told him I'd broken my neck years before, stressing that, for me, it's a *privilege* to run. Coincidentally, Reynaldo was recovering from a calf injury after being a professional basketball player for the Cuban National Team, although he no longer played with the team. Reynaldo said he needed to run early so he could be at work at a pizzeria by nine.

That day on the Malecón, I ran stronger than on my other runs. Meeting Reynaldo reminded me we can use more than words to connect two cultures.

# BEST SOUVENIR– RECIPE FOR COCONUT NATILLA

Keeping the roadways, airways, and waterways hot, I still had time to bring back souvenirs. I have my fair share of art, T-shirts, CDs, jewelry, and knickknacks; some would call me a well-traveled pack rat. However, the absolute best souvenirs from my travels are tasty and don't break the bank. That's right. I bring back recipes, including the cancháncharas and mojitos already noted. Recipes take up little space in my luggage or home. Plus, I can share my stories with friends and family around a table with this souvenir as the highlight.

Over my years in Cuba, I have consumed kilos of roasted pork and of course plenty of Cuban rum, cigars, and coffee. Here's a custard-like dessert that two wonderful women, Daylene and Cuqui, shared with me. You'll find their coconut natilla a creamy, tropical delight that's easy to make.

## RECIPE FOR COCONUT NATILLA

Prep time: 10 minutes
Cook time: 25–30 minutes
Total time: 35–40 minutes

Ingredients:

1. 8 egg yolks (*yema de huevos*)
2. 2 cups whole milk (*leche*)
3. 4 tsp. cornstarch (diluted into ½ cup of water) *(maicena)*
4. 1 tsp. coconut flavoring *(sabor de coco)*
5. 1 stick of cinnamon and ground cinnamon for finished natilla *(canela)*
6. ¼ tsp. salt *(sal)*
7. 1½ cup sugar *(azúcar)*

Instructions:

- Bring milk, salt, cinnamon stick, and coconut flavor to a boil.
- Remove from heat and let the mixture decrease to room temperature.
- Mix eggs, sugar, and diluted cornstarch in a separate bowl.
- Once the milk mixture has cooled, mix all together. (Remove the cinnamon stick.)
- Place the combined mixture on the stove and bring to medium heat until thick.
- Dish the thickened natilla into a serving bowl or 4 separate serving dishes, sprinkle with ground cinnamon, and chill.

A big thank you to my two Cuban friends in Playa Larga on the Bay of Pigs who often prepared this dessert for me. I miss you both. With this recipe, I have a way to relive and share my Cuban travel memories anytime.

Warning: Don't expect leftovers. When in doubt, make two natillas.

**CHPTR 19**

# GUANTANAMERA

The "Guantanamera" song can be heard around the world. You can most certainly recall its refrain:

*Guantanamera, guajira guantanamera*
*Guantanamera, guajira, guantanamera*

Most assume the song is of Mexican origin because of the mariachi bands that play it in addition to "La Bamba" and "Besame Mucho." However, let me debunk that misconception started over a pitcher of margaritas eons ago.

"Guantanamera" is a Cuban song—one of the most patriotic Cuban songs with lyrics written by José Martí, national hero and poet. Martí is a symbol of Cuba's independence against the Spanish. Without a doubt, when in Cuba, you will see monuments and tributes to him everywhere. In Havana, the Revolution Square pays homage to José Martí as well as a statue pointing at the U.S. Embassy on Havana's Malecón. However, across the country from Guantanamo in the East to the tobacco region of Pinar del Rio in the West, statues of José Martí can be found in front of almost all schools and educational facilities.

With almost every strolling musician in Cuba cued up to play "Guantanamera," guests often ask, "What is a Guantanamera, anyway?" In a combo Spanish and geography lesson, I explain by asking this dumb question: "Have you heard of Guantanamo?" Of course! Just about everyone who's been paying attention to the global War on Terrorism knows of Guantanamo (or Gitmo), the U.S. naval base in Cuba. Since an amendment written at the beginning of the 20th century, the U.S. has leased a piece of eastern Cuba for a naval base. This has been and continues to be a big thorn in Cuba's side. Imagine the resentment of having an enemy country that's placed a sixty-year embargo on your own *patria* (homeland) hosting a military base on your land. That takes some *cojones* (balls)!

Don't forget that, in addition to the military base, there's a Cuban province named Guantanamo. A person from this province can be a *guantanamero* (male) or a *guantanamera* (female), depending on gender. So, the song "Guantanamera" is about a girl from the Guantanamo countryside.

The next time you hear it, remember that it's Cuban music and should be accompanied with a rum drink. Perhaps a rum and Coke cocktail called a *Cubalibre* (Free Cuba) would be appropriate!

# BIG CHANGES AFLOAT

Six months into my New Year's Resolution, I had escaped my Cubicle Land and made my office mobile. I spent half the month in Cuba and the remaining time in South Florida. While on the road, I had little time to write except for a postcard or a page or two in my journal. When in Florida, I dedicated most of my time to retelling my adventures as well as researching how I could get my first memoir published. I already had the title, *When All Balls Drop*, and had registered the domain name. Coincidentally, this book didn't have anything to do with travel. It's the story that led up to starting Life 2.0.

As I transitioned out of the corporate world, my PIC was also looking for a change. He'd been flying helicopters in BFE (Bum F*** Egypt) Louisiana for the oil industry. But he sought a full-time, pilot position in a place both of us would enjoy. Being big dreamers, we joked around about living on a tropical island before we were forty.

Hey, if you dream it, it will come, right? And it did!

On June 13th, I was using the only computer in our Havana hotel (hidden beneath the lobby stairs) to write my mother a happy birthday message. I pressed "send" and, at the same time, I received an email from Brian. My PIC had an offer to fly tours in Hawaii, specifically Kauai. His job would start in two weeks. "So when can you move out?" he wrote. Needless to say, I replied back, "Congrats. I'll see you on my break in August. I can move after my last tour this year."

With this type of life-changing news, I'd typically be on the phone with my clan sharing his awesome new job and our move to paradise. However, I didn't get that chance until I returned later that week. Yes, I'd be moving to Kauai. Woo-hoo! I didn't think my guests in Cuba would like to hear this news. Still, I had to share it.

As the group and I boarded the *guagua* (bus) with a full day of sites and activities planned, I sat beside Yislaine. She noticed I had a mischievous smile. Our first stop was Revolution Square where Fidel Castro had given his marathon speeches and Pope John Paul II had held mass. As our guests got out of the bus to take photos of the José Martí memorial and two facades of revolutionary heroes, Che Guevara and Camilo Cienfuegos, I looked at my soul sister, Yislaine, and said, "I have a secret to tell you."

Knowing that I loved games and had a good sense of humor, she hesitated a moment. "Okay. Then tell me."

"I'm moving. Instead of saying *hola*, I'm going to say *aloha*."

Yislaine was happy, but I could tell she felt concerned that I wouldn't come back to Cuba. I reassured her that the move wouldn't happen until the end of the year. Little did I know that later, Yislaine would surprise me with a secret, too.

# CUBA OPENS DOORS TO THE WORLD

Shortly after I decided to move to Hawaii, it was Cuba that provided the connection to keep traveling a component of my career. I had already followed the advice of experts who said that, in any industry, it's wise to "play nice" in the sandbox with the competition and your peers. "You never know if or when they may be your colleagues or even a boss," they say. I've seen this play out writing books, freelancing, and leading tours.

This certainly was the case on a tour from hell in Cuba, which led to a surprising job offer. On this particular tour, we experienced hiccup after hiccup after hiccup. For example, we lost our first day in Cuba because of charter flight delays in Miami. The owner of the specialized travel agency, Wendi, a confident blonde in her early fifties with a Midwestern accent, came to my guests' welcoming meeting. She booked her clients with my employer, a tour operator with the legal license for people-to-people tours in Cuba for Americans. Naturally, Wendi wanted to help ease their concerns when I broke this first piece of bad news to them: on the first day, we would tour Little Havana in Hialeah, Florida, instead of Old Havana in Cuba because of delays with the charter. She requested I update her throughout the trip, which would be limited due to lack of Internet service. However, I promised to copy her on all itinerary changes and essential communications I'd send to my headquarters.

## ROOMMATE ISSUES

On this tour from hell, after everyone on the tour arrived in Cuba, we had typical hotel room, water, and menu complications. However, the biggest hiccup was roommate issues. Some guests who didn't know one another opted to share a room with a stranger of the same gender to make the trip more affordable. One woman was a night owl paired with an early bird needing an hour in the bathroom before breakfast. Another accused the other of using all the toiletries while her roommate's rebuttal was she snored. It turned out to be like summer camp all over again. So I put on my Heidi Camp Counselor hat and asked about options for additional rooms to accommodate those complaining. Nope, no vacancy. Next, it was mediating their differences. Who needed bathroom time in the morning versus in the evening? Was one of the roommates willing to sleep in my room instead? However, the final hiccup became the tipping point. On the charter flight return, we were delayed for more than three hours. This made most of our guests miss their connecting flights home out of Miami. Not a good finale to a trip!

Although I had to jump into many Plan B's along the way—especially the impromptu tour of Little Havana on day one and a *Cubalibre* party at the airport on the last day—my customer service ratings and tips were still stellar.

## FROM CUBA TO PERU?

Back in Florida from Cuba and before my next tour there *and* my inaugural trip to the Garden Isle of Kauai, I received a message from Wendi. She complimented my performance with her group and asked if I worked for other companies. I explained, "I work for only one company so I can have time to dedicate to writing." Then Wendi said her travel company needed someone who spoke Spanish to escort a tour to Peru in the fall. Would I be interested? This tour included Lima, Cuzco, and Machu Picchu, one of the seven new wonders of the world.

What a carrot she was dangling in front of me! I dearly wanted to return to Peru. After sleeping on it, I considered the difficulties I'd face dealing with back-to-back tours to a familiar country (Cuba) followed by an unfamiliar country (Peru). And although the people speak the same language, the two countries differ in almost every aspect: food, topography, DNA, and more.

## REGARDLESS, I TOOK THE BAIT.

The Peru tour challenged me for sure. But it also opened the door for my move to Hawaii. Wendi's travel agency offered worldwide tours and needed my honed skills as a dependable tour director. I could do it, although my office would change. It wouldn't be Cuba and South Florida; it would be Kauai as well as various familiar and exotic new places. In fact, after my move to Hawaii,

I led trips to Peru, New Zealand, Australia, Greece, Spain, Italy, Morocco, Portugal, and the Hawaiian Islands.

How could an island in the Caribbean that's been isolated for decades lead to my seeing the world? This is why fact is stranger than fiction. And if my stories were fiction, they would have to make sense. Hollywood couldn't make this stuff up!

# THE CONVERSATION I WILL NEVER FORGET
## [JULY 26, 2013]

After umpteen visits to Cuba, the country and its people still continue to amaze me. Many argue that Cuban people's perseverance, sense of community, and ingenuity are the nation's biggest strengths. I agree with them; however, I feel the Cubans' approach to happiness is by far paramount. It is my greatest takeaway from being in this wonderful country. That's why I share this unforgettable conversation about a rooster.

On July 26, 2013, I had the opportunity to speak to José Fuster, a world-renowned Cuban artist of mosaics and paintings. I sat beside him at the pool in his home, an ornate three-floor playground of colorful mosaics and statues nicknamed Fusterlandia. Seated together underneath his mosaic of the patron saint of Cuba, *Nuestra Señora de la Caridad del Cobre* (Our Lady of Charity of Copper), I asked him, "What's the rooster all about? It appears in all of your work as if it's your signature."

Dangling his feet in the water while enjoying a Cristal beer, Fuster explained that he cherishes the sound of the *gallo*. When he hears its morning crowing, he knows he's blessed with yet another day.

## CELEBRATING LIFE EACH DAY

When I heard José's spin on what most would call a loud, shrilling cry of a rooster, I reflected on how right he is. Celebrating life each and every day—taking time to #LookUp—is extremely crucial to enjoying a happy life. These simple principles often fall by the wayside in the time-pressed grind of daily living.

I had this unforgettable conversation before I moved to Kauai, which has an overpopulation of roosters. So when the neighborhood roosters (aka island alarm clocks) crow at three in the morning, I remember Fuster's message to enjoy each cock-a-doodle-doo with gratitude.

Here's to looking up and always hearing the cock-a-doodle-doo as a reminder to be grateful.

# CHPTR 23

# ALOHA 101– A PREVIEW OF KAUAI

On break from my tours to Cuba, I packed up for a four-week preview of Kauai. Arriving late evening, Brian greeted me with a purple and white lei and drove me to our *ohana* (mother-in-law's quarters). Located in the principal city on Kauai, our house was in Lihue proper only minutes from the airport, beach, and *the* store on the island, Costco. Our *ohana* comprised of only a bedroom, bathroom, living room, and kitchen, but that didn't matter. Living in Hawaii before we were forty years old was our dream. We have a home on a tropical island!

Brian took the liberty of decorating this *ohana*, which on a remote island is tricky and expensive. The once-white bare walls were covered with pastel paintings of shells and flowers as well as scenes of native Hawaiian ceremonies and dances. If I didn't know better, I would have thought I had checked into a 1990s hotel room.

Regardless, it was ours—or at least for the first night.

On day two, a pair of Brian's friends came and crashed on our couch. Let this be a warning for those planning to live in paradise. Your friends come out of the woodwork. Albeit a little too soon to have visitors, still, it was fun to have them do some exploring with me while Brian was flying circles around the Garden Isle. Plus, they bought us a housewarming gift, our first set of guest towels and sheets.

Like any first-time visitor, I headed up to the North Shore to view beautiful Hanalei Beach as well as hike the beginning of the Kalalau Trail called Hanakapiai Trail. Also, I became obsessed with all of the roosters. Like a rooster paparazzi, I took photos of them every chance I got. On Kauai, chickens and roosters are everywhere: at the beach, on the hiking trails, at Wal-Mart, and even at the airport.

After our guests left, I flew with my PIC around the island in a chopper, reminding me of our first date in South Florida three years previously. Little did we know then that my helicopter flight lesson with him as my instructor would lead to years of adventuring together. Although many are scared of flying in a helicopter, I find it to be far smoother than any airplane experience I've ever taken. Kauai by helicopter is, bar none, the best way to see the island. Some parts of the island don't have roads, and people can only get there by hiking, kayaking, or bushwhacking.

I also made time to get my residency handled, switching over my driver's license, and networking with professionals in Hawaiian travel, tourism, and writing. Although I wouldn't be officially moving for another four months, it was essential to put out feelers in advance. Some showed me *aloha* and others not so much as I was a *haule* (mainlander). Over that month, I started to study the basic Hawaiian language, but after about thirty words, I stopped. I didn't connect with it like I did Spanish, plus, as a global tour manager, wouldn't my time be better used learning Mandarin or Arabic?

Regardless of not feeling the need to learn Hawaiian, I did connect deeply to the word *aloha* and the phrase *live aloha*. You might know *aloha* simply as hello or goodbye, but it's so much more. At its core, *aloha* describes a state of mind or behavior that encourages everyone to be loving, patient, in tune with nature, and appreciating the moment.

If you've read my previous books and are familiar with the mantra #LookUp and #LookUpDay, you know why I immediately connected with *aloha*. With #LookUp's two components of "being in the moment" and "finding the upside of any situation," it fits naturally with *living aloha*.

Yes, all signs were pointing toward writing my first book in Kauai.

## CUBAN CONNECTION IN KAUAI–KAYAKING NA PALI

With a distance of more than eight thousand miles between Cuba and Kauai, some amazing similarities struck me on my first summer on the Garden Island. First and foremost, many of the plants are the same. The red blooms of poinciana trees, massive banyan trees, and an array of hibiscus in every color are the same as in Cuba. So are many of the fruits including mangos, guavas, and papayas. However, the island has distinct sweet fruits

I tasted for the first time in Kauai: lilikoi (passion fruit), longon, and hairy rambutan (both types of lychee). I wagered they would grow in Cuba but hadn't seen them.

The second similarity between the two islands is the love of pork. Even a novice of Cuban cuisine and culture knows that pork is fabulous, succulent, and the national dish. And the same holds true for Hawaii. Perhaps the marinades of both cultures are different, but the same slow-roasted method is used whether in a *caja china* (a BBQ box which literally translates to Chinese box) or an *imu* (underground earth oven) in Hawaii.

The third commonality is island time. Compared to the pace of the Mainland (continental United States), Hawaii takes it slow. There is no "in a New York minute" pace in Hawaii. That wouldn't be *aloha*.

However, *aloha* island time is still not like in the Caribbean, and Cuba takes the cake. There, living in the moment, not being in a rush, and watching the world go by are a part of Cuban life. With all these similarities, I knew the world was small. I was bound to run into a Cuban in Kauai. It was not until my best adventure of that first summer that I met Kique. Both Kique and his brother had been born in Cuba and emigrated to the States decades ago. To respect their privacy, I didn't ask about their particular journey of coming to America. I suspected from their age, late fifties, they were Marielitos who had flooded Miami in 1980. Coming to Kauai after stays in Alaska and other parts of the U.S., they settled on the North Shore of Kauai to open the only kayak rental and tour company at the time. It was with Kique's company that both Brian and I first paddled the eighteen-mile long North Shore of Kauai, the Na Pali Coast.

Starting before rooster crow, we drove to the North Shore to meet the crew and get our gear. By 6 a.m. we were off to the launching site that was near the end of the road as the Na Pali Coast isn't accessible via car. Access is only along one long, precarious hike called the Kalalau Trail or via boat. Kauai's North Shore is world-renowned, one of the most beautiful mountain coastlines on the planet. What makes it pristine is also what makes it hard to experience up close and personal. It remains relatively untapped because of limited access due to lack of roads and dangerous winter swells.

Given that the time of year for safely kayaking down the Na Pali is summer, we were in luck. Although we kayaked with the currents, it wasn't a walk in the park. Brian and I were by far the strongest paddlers in the group, but even in our tandem kayak with a rudder, it took both of us constant, synchronized effort. Previously, we had contemplated doing the kayak trip alone, but neither one of us knew the landscape well. Brian knew only about caves that were accessible via kayak, but not exactly where, how dangerous, and how to gauge the tight enclosures. We made the right decision to join a group for our maiden voyage down the Na Pali.

From the moment the sun rose, it was like kayaking through a postcard. The ocean near the cliffs was an inviting aqua while the deeper waters were a mysterious dark blue. This intense color palette contrasted beautifully with the volcanic cliffs and lush green valleys along the coast.

Following the lead of our guide, Kique's nephew, we entered a large cave that had an open ceiling. He suggested this would be a resting point out of the waves, wind, and current. Once inside, both Brian and I jumped out of the kayak to cool off and take a needed pee break. Only mid-morning, we were just a third of the way to Polihale Beach on the west side of the island. The guide reminded us that the next big milestone would be the view of Kalalau Valley and Beach. I couldn't have imagined better scenery than what we'd already witnessed, but it just kept coming, valley after valley with their secret waterfalls, then Kalalau's expansive beach. Following that was a beach with an archway I learned was in the 1998 movie *Six Days Seven Nights* with Harrison Ford and Anne Heche.

It was hard to fathom we had all of this beauty practically to ourselves. Traveling in a pack of five kayaks, we only met one catamaran, a handful of fishermen, and some locals in a Zodiac boat. But then again, this route is not for queasy stomachs or those afraid of the ocean with or without motor.

After seeing some of the Kalalau hikers with packs, I commented to Brian, "I'd like to do that, too. I want to see this same area, but from a different vantage point, with new eyes." And we got a chance to do that.

# CUBAN CONNECTION IN WISCONSIN— FLASHBACK TO DAD'S GARAGE

One fall evening in 1980, my father received a call at our hobby farm in Galesville, Wisconsin. An officer from the La Crosse police department asked about Dad's property on Vine Street in town close to the university. After verifying my father was indeed renting out two apartments in the house, the male officer inquired, "Mr. Siefkas, do you know you have people living in your garage, too?"

"No, I wasn't aware of people living there."

"This evening, we noticed lights on in the garage, so we knocked and found two recent Cuban immigrants setting up mattresses."

"Well, I'd be happy to rent it to them."

"We'll let you handle that. Tonight, we'll ask them to leave."

Little did my dad know that in that year, 1980, more than a hundred thousand Cubans immigrated to the United States. In waves between April and October, Castro allowed Cubans to go freely to the United States if their families brought boats from Florida to Cuba. However, the one stipulation was that if they took family members, they'd also have to take others. The "others" were mental health patients and criminals. This produced a disastrous tent city under Miami's I-95 overpass. Those in the Cuban community opened their homes to family members as well as others in need, but apparently many of them weren't healthy or were destined for a criminal life in their new country.

Those Cubans never tried to squat in Dad's Vine Street garage again. However, we learned they were part of the wave of thousands of Cuban immigrants called *Marielitos*—those who left Cuba from the Port of Mariel in 1980.

I wonder what drew the *Marielitos* to Wisconsin—short summers, long winters, or an affinity for cheese. It certainly wasn't for the lutefisk or polka. (Although I love cheese, brats, and even own a Cheesehead hat, I can take my Wisconsin roots only so far. I've never been fond of the accordion and won't touch lutefisk with a ten-foot pole.) I think Kique and his brother were smart in their choice of Kauai over Wisconsin. Although Little Havana and Miami are home to close to a million Cubans, Kauai is as close to Cuba in climate, flora, fauna, and lifestyle in the U.S. as one can get today.

# LOOK UP DAY FROM 11,000 FEET

On this particular Look Up Day, September 27th, 2013—exactly four years after my freak tree accident that sparked a life change and the mantra #LookUp—I found myself in Cusco, Peru, at more than eleven thousand feet in elevation. My only experience with elevation in the past had been hiking the Rocky Mountains, which produced intense headaches and racing heartbeat. However, that trip was personal and the elevation was less than Peru. This trip to Cusco and eventually Machu Picchu was for work, so I was not only responsible for myself but two dozen guests. I suspected my highly active body would take to the elevation, but I needed to be prepared.

I did my research and visited my general practitioner in Florida to get a prescription for elevation sickness pills. Although I prefer not to pill pop, I had to ensure I'd have the best odds of being functional. I know the Incas treated elevation sickness with coca leaves and many tourists swear by coca tea, but I wanted something surefire. Remember that I lived in Lihue, Kauai, at two hundred feet above sea level and South Florida where the elevation can be below ten feet. As directed, I started taking the medication the day prior to flying to Cusco and would continue until our return to Lima after both Cusco and Machu Picchu.

I met my group in Lima two days before flying to Cusco. Never loving the congested, large dirty cities of South America, I wished we had just continued to Cusco directly. However, the day in Lima allowed us to gradually adjust to time zone and altitude changes, and being with the group. Their ages ranged from mid-forties to a woman celebrating her seventy-fifth birthday on the trip.

We arrived at the Cusco airport among the Inca dancers and musicians who greeted us. As soon as I could, I made a beeline for the *coca* tea table and suggested the same for my group.

## TOUR OF CUSCO

After meeting our local guide, a Peruvian bodybuilder with a heavy, hard-to-understand accent, we started our tour of Cusco, including two Incan ruins, the Plaza Mayor, and the Cathedral, all before lunch. Caught up in logistics with the guide as well as taking in Cusco for the first time myself, I didn't feel the effects of the elevation in the bus. In our first stop at Quricancha (Coricancha), an Inca temple in Cusco proper, I entered the historic site with the group. But within minutes of a little physical activity, I needed to sit. I felt lightheaded, my heart raced, and

80

a piercing headache surfaced. As I've shared, there's nothing like traveler's diarrhea to put you right in the moment, but elevation sickness does the trick, too!

There was little I could do except take in lots of water, continue with the medication, drink coca tea, and take breaks. I informed our local guide about my situation; no one else in the group would pay attention to my whereabouts or wellbeing. That's the catch with being the tour manager; you're supposed to be the bionic leader with an immune system of steel. You are the mother hen, but who's your mother?

With time, more coca tea, and lunch, I got my wits about me, but I wasn't going to push it. From our last stop for the day, Saksaywaman (pronounced like sexy woman), an Inca citadel and a Cusco overlook, I reveled in feeling as normal as someone can feel at eleven thousand feet instead of at sea level.

## HAPPY LOOK UP DAY

This day could be celebrated as a Happy Look Up Day for two reasons: 1) I was certainly forced to live in the moment and be mindful of my body and 2) I also needed to spin the situation positively. Here I was in Cusco, Peru. I had recovered from my broken neck of four years earlier, and I was living an adventurous Life 2.0.

Here's to looking up!

# SUNRISE HIKE IN MACHU PICCHU

Although I'm a morning person who loves a good sunrise, whoever came up with the addition of sunrise hikes or bicycle rides to travel itineraries must have been an insomniac. Regardless of the place, whether Diamondhead in Honolulu or Machu Picchu in Peru, in order to get to the trailhead or entrance before the sunrise and then hike to your viewing point, you have to get up in the middle of the night.

My most memorable sunrise hike was at Machu Picchu. At four in the morning, I awoke in my hotel room to heavy rain outside. From our conversations the night before, I knew that only eight of my nearly thirty guests wanted to see the sunrise. I was hedging my bets that, with the rain, no one would show up in the lobby at four-thirty. But they surprised me. For some reason when on holiday, even people who are slow as molasses and dread mornings force themselves out of bed to witness a sunrise in a foreign country. Would they ever get out of bed before seven or eight at home? I doubt it!

Still drizzling and dark, eight of us carefully walked to the bus stop over the slick cobblestone streets of Aguas Calientes and lined up with twenty other travelers. It looked like we'd make the cut-off for the first bus up the mountain at five-thirty. It would take us to the entrance of Machu Picchu, which opened at six. Within minutes of our arrival, the line grew to fifty people deep.

We had purchased our round-trip tickets from a small kiosk just minutes before the bus pulled up. A little wet and wearing raingear, we'd be sitting stuck to another person for the bumpy fifteen-minute ride up the hill. With just enough seats available for our group of eight, we sat wherever available and next to whomever.

The bus arrived at the entrance about ten minutes before Machu Picchu's entrance was to open. The rain had stopped, but heavy cloud cover remained, and we hoped for an improvement in another thirty minutes. As the security guards opened the gates, I led my group to the Sun Temple, a high east-facing structure close to Huayna Picchu. We waited there for the sunrise, perched on stones eating small bags of breakfast the hotel had prepared for us.

## BEHIND THE CLOUDS

Indeed, the sun did rise, but behind the clouds—a sunless sunrise. That wasn't necessarily what my guests expected at Machu Picchu, but more often than not, the morning is cloudy at that site.

Still, I was delighted, regardless of this imperfect sunrise. The clouds lingering around the surrounding mountains made the view surreal, almost like a fantasy. Plus, it was the most private experience we'd had at Machu Picchu. Two hours later, Machu Picchu resembled a colony of ants with tour groups tripping over tour groups in every language imaginable.

Maybe that insomniac had some reason to suggest sunrise hikes and bikes. The hordes don't come out for sunrises, especially when it's cloudy and rainy.

## CHPTR 27

# FRIENDS IN CUBA
# SAVE THE DAY

Upon returning to Cuba, after my inaugural visit to Kauai and my tour to Peru, I started to tell my Cuban friends I'd be moving to Hawaii at the end of the year. Although we had known each other only a short time, the time we spent together had been intense. My friends in Cienfuegos helped me turn rooming and water fiascos into solvable problems. They had become my therapists after a long day with the group, listening to my tales and making me mojitos. Likewise, I listened to their stories about love gone wrong or dreams of traveling themselves, giving advice when they wanted it and just being a friend with a good ear. Each time I came to Cuba, I brought items that made their lives easier and healthier. I knew I was going to miss them and they me.

## AN ODD TRIP

My last tour in Cuba that year, 2013, was in early December. From the first night I met my group in Miami, I had a feeling from its make-up I'd have an odd trip. Nearly half of the people knew one another from a professional mental health organization and had an alpha woman group leader, Karol. The remaining guests were all baby boomer couples. In fact, one of the wives, Lynn from California, was a repeat traveler. She and her girlfriend from college had traveled with me on my training trip. I vaguely remembered Lynn having mood swings like a manic depressive, and while she was with her friend, Lynn didn't ruffle anyone's feathers except her own. Although it started out well with Lynn as my cheerleader, this time I sensed she expected preferential treatment because she had traveled with me before.

This group dynamic, in combination with working with a newbie guide instead of Yislaine, was disappointing. In fact, this trip to Cuba was just as challenging as my first solo tour. I should have known better. Tours never get easier; there are just more predictable obstacles and a greater comfort improvising solutions.

This was true on a free evening in Cienfuegos. I had arranged a reservation for half the group. Karol, the alpha, had already researched a *paladar* (private restaurant) online where she wanted to go. Neither our guide nor I had been there; thus, I recommended against a place that neither of us knew. Instead, I suggested she and her group join us at the rooftop terrace *paladar*. She wasn't having it. Karol wanted it her way. So the guide called to make reservations for Karol's group. Trusting that our guide had done her part, I joined the other half of the group to walk them to the restaurant and dine.

Not more than fifteen minutes after sitting at our table, the other group entered with Karol heading right for me. She immediately, without any pleasantries, yelled, "You sent us to a closed restaurant!" I excused myself from the table to get the full story. Apparently as they were trying to find the restaurant Karol wanted, one of the group members asked a young man for directions. Whether it was lost in translation or a way for the possible *jinetero* (shady character) to drive business to a friend's place, the young man said the restaurant they were looking for was closed. Karol was fuming mad. They didn't continue walking to double-check if it actually was closed, but they did see my recommended restaurant across the street.

Without more than "I'm so sorry. Let me fix this," I immediately got the owner and head waitress to set up additional tables for another ten to join us, but Karol didn't want to out of spite. Although I hadn't recommended the location, nor was I with the group to ascertain the restaurant was closed, she blamed me for her failed plan. Eventually, her husband calmed her, convincing Karol this was the best Plan B. It was yet another reminder that going with online or travel book recommendations aren't always the best way to plan a trip. I learned that travel lesson the hard way when I ended up in a brothel on Christmas in Turkey in '97. (See Travel Lesson: Trust Your Gut More than the Guide Books.)

## GOOD DOSES OF FRIENDSHIP

The following day, Sunday afternoon, a good dose of friendship was what I needed. And my Cuban friends threw me a birthday party! It was an outstanding surprise. My November birthday had been two weeks earlier, but I hadn't been in Cuba then. Maylene, my confidante and head therapist in Cienfuegos, called me to the hotel terrace where fifteen of my friends and their family members sat at a large table set up with bottles of rum, Tu Kola (Cuba's version of Coke), glasses, ice, and a large birthday cake with candles. They sang "Feliz Cumpleaños" with an encore of "Happy Birthday." I was touched. Not only wasn't I expecting it, but I *needed* it. A good dose of friendship goes a long way in getting through tough times.

## LIKE A BULLDOG

In fact, I needed another dose on this trip. That's when, as my gut suspected, Lynn unleashed her demons. It was midday in Old Havana's Plaza Vieja. I was counting to see if everyone had returned from free time for bathrooms, pictures, coffee, or other. Almost like a bulldog, she yelled at me in front of the entire group, "You're a narcissist Nazi." Lynn continued to insult and accuse me of manipulating the schedule for my own ulterior motives; meanwhile, people in the group stood speechless. I immediately apologized, saying, "I'm so sorry for making you feel unhappy at any point in the tour. You have to know that it wasn't intentional. I promise to do anything in my capability to turn this around for you." But she said, "There's nothing you can do."

Given there was no reason to draw more attention to the tirade, I recounted the group, double-checked with the *compay* system, and off we went to lunch. I let our local guide lead the group while I pulled up the rear. In this position, I had various tagalongs sympathizing with me, adding their two cents about Lynn's mood swings and just stating, "I think you're doing a spectacular job."

After another three days of keeping the group as happy and healthy as possible while walking on eggshells around Lynn and Karol, I was beat. Overall, the group had an unforgettable time, but the trip wasn't the finale I had envisioned. At the Havana airport, I assisted everyone through check-in and waited for the last two, Lynn and her husband, to go through security and export tax. Before proceeding myself, I saw a familiar smiling face. It was Yislaine wearing her blue work shirt from her assignment.

We hugged and talked for a few minutes before we both needed to go. I shared Lynn's insults as well as the birthday party in Cienfuegos. Neither of us knew when we'd see each other again. We both started to cry. As I stepped forward to pass through security and passport control, I promised to send her my finished book. That dose of friendship was the perfect finale to a year in Cuba.

# CHPTR 28

# MY MOVE TO THE GARDEN ISLE

Packing for a trip to Kauai is a lot different than moving to Kauai, the Garden Isle in Hawaii. And moving to Kauai is a lot different than moving to another state in the Continental U.S. of A.

On previous moves from Massachusetts to South Florida, I had rented a U-Haul with a car in tow. Not this time. I shipped dozens of boxes via the slow boat, packed two suitcases for the plane, and sold my Honda Limo. I knew I could buy everything I needed on Kauai even though I'd pay a premium.

Packing up box after box of my books convinced me I needed to start reading e-books and perhaps even explore audio books. Seriously, more boxes of books were shipped than anything else. Other items that took about a month and a half to get to Kauai were my SCUBA gear, hat collection (yes, I have a box full of hats), and bulky clothes and shoes. My advice for anyone moving to the Hawaiian Islands: be minimalistic. I brought and shipped too much!

Selling my Honda Limo was easy—a quick call to family friends in Wisconsin who had purchased my dad's last car. They heard "low-mileage Honda, stick shift, and roof racks." SOLD. Before my last tour to Cuba, these friends flew to Florida from Wisconsin and drove the car back home. The end of an era.

For the actual flight to Hawaii, I didn't travel light. As carry-ons, I brought only essentials: my MacBook and my roller board (aka mobile file cabinet with last seven years of taxes, divorce decree, birth certificate, and journals from my accident through to my recovery). The suitcases borderlined on oversized and overweight. Although I packed primarily summer clothes, I was expecting to continue traveling so I needed winter gear as well as my touring uniforms, signs, and banners.

After the fifteen hours and multiple legs of my final move flight, I was destroyed. I'd just come back from my emotional trip to Cuba, packed up what remained of my life in Florida, and said farewells to my friends as well as my dad. Once again, Brian greeted me with a purple and white lei at the airport and, as promised, a chilled bottle of wine at our *ohana*. No visitors for at least three months. *Our* paradise at last.

## ROUGH DRAFT AND ROOSTERS

That holiday season, I learned to say *Mele Kelikimaka* (Merry Christmas in Hawaiian) and began writing toward meeting an aggressive goal—publishing my first book in nine months. I set up my Kauai office out of our bedroom. On a TV dinner tray next to our bed, I converted my journal entries from my Special

Period. It was like my college days when I'd study from a walk-in closet that had a fan to cover ambient noise. Thankfully, this small bedroom with a window AC drowned out the Kauai roosters.

The common myth about roosters is that they crow at daybreak; however, let me demystify it—at least for the Kauai roosters. Yes, they crow in the morning (thus the nickname Kauai alarm clock), but they also crow at all hours. Around our *ohana*, I used earplugs (aka chicken plugs) to sleep past 4:00 a.m.

Regardless of my intending to write, drinking massive quantities of Kauai coffee, and even having the house to myself, I got stalled. With only three months before my next tour Down Under, I couldn't afford any time to suffer writer's block! But instead of pushing through and writing "crap," I chose to tap into the environment and use it to my advantage.

I packed up for a dose of *aloha* and adventure.

Whether an afternoon on my stand-up paddleboard or another office with a view of the ocean, I wrote in places all over Kauai— at the coffee shop down the street, on the treadmill at the gym, on the bike trail in Kapa'a, and certainly on my hikes. And the roosters accompanied me as well as Fuster's wisdom.

## OHANA VISITORS

Guess who was our first visitor after my move to Kauai? My dad. It wasn't his first trip to the Garden Isle. Several years earlier, he had visited two friends he knew from teaching theatre and speech at the University of Wisconsin in LaCrosse. When Brian and I told him we were moving to Kauai, he smiled and said, "If I were your age, I'd do it in a heartbeat. It is such a beautiful place."

By the time my father arrived, I had finished the first draft, and was rereading and tweaking my manuscript. Little did he know he would be put to work; there's no free room and board in Kauai. His multiple hours a day in front of the TV watching news and political shows would be exchanged for proofreading *When All Balls Drop*. (Besides, we didn't have TV.)

He had planned his trip to occur before my tour Down Under as well as to coincide with visits from family friends Matt and Carol. They are the couple in their late-sixties who had introduced him to Winter, Wisconsin, and Black Dan Lake. He owes Matt and Carol for the idea of buying the cabin at Black Dan Lake, which he later sold to my dear childhood friend Adriana and her family.

The timing of their visit was perfect. It came when I needed to set my manuscript aside so I could look at it later with new eyes. Also, I had been on the island for nearly three months. It was certainly time to put on my tour director hat.

## WAILUA RIVER FUN AND QUEEN'S BATH

Even before I was born, Matt, Carol, Mom, and Dad had canoed and kayaked down Wisconsin rivers, so it seemed only fitting we do the same on their visit. With our kayak nicknamed Corky (because we used a wine cork as a stopper) loaded in the back of our truck, Carol and I sat in the cab with the cooler. Meanwhile, my dad and Matt got comfortable in the bed of the truck—Hawaiian style—and we headed to the Wailua River. After renting another kayak, the four of us assumed the position of leisure kayakers with a cooler full of beer and snacks. This amazing river valley became our backdrop for stories of float trips gone wrong and canoe tippings on Black Dan Lake or the Black

93

River near my hometown. Anyone on the Wailua River that day knew we were coming; all of our stories were punctuated by Matt's contagious laughter.

On another day's adventure, we headed to the North Shore for a short hike to a natural tide pool called Queen's Bath, which overlooks Hanalei Bay. The quarter mile hike down wasn't a problem for any of us (unless getting muddy is an issue, for all hikes in Kauai are muddy). However, we took the steep incline going up very slowly. On the return trip, my father fatigued quickly, needing to stop for numerous breaks to recuperate from shortness of breath. This was unlike him, an active gym goer for fifty years. Carol and Matt waited for Dad and me at the top. Then Matt took me aside and said, "I think he should go see a doctor. This isn't normal for him."

After this visit, both my dad and I had homework. I had revisions to do on my manuscript; he had to visit his doctor for a checkup.

| C U B A | CHPTR 29 |
|---------|----------|

# IF SOMEONE JUMPS OFF A BRIDGE, WOULD YOU JUMP, TOO?

After moving to Hawaii, my tours happened quarterly as I headed for destinations that made sense for my physical location as well as my expertise. The first was a three-and-a-half week cruise and land tour of New Zealand and Australia. I had never traveled to either country, but at least I wouldn't have a language barrier.

This tour included fifty guests, far too many for one tour manager to handle. Thus, I co-led the tour with a newbie, Eve, who was a friend of the owner. It was a daunting task to lead a tour to a new destination. But add to that the sheer number of people, combined with working with someone who is a friend of the owner, Wendi, oh my. And it gets better. Eve and I weren't only co-leaders of the tour; we were also roommates. Yeppers, we had to squeeze ourselves into a small stateroom cabin: two women + one bathroom = #@!*

Given this set-up, she and I wouldn't get any breaks from each other. I knew it would be the most challenging tour yet: eighteen-hour days, sleepless nights, seasickness, and roommate conflicts. What could I do to kick off the tour with optimism and shift my perspective of this multiple-week grand feat?

## AN ADVENTURE PRESENTS ITSELF

Weeks before the tour started, Wendi contacted me after a request from two guests arriving in Auckland a day early. Both wanted to bungee jump, and they extended the invitation to others who would also arrive early. Knowing my personality well, Wendi presented the opportunity to me while indicating it would be excellent marketing for her company. Yes, she was okay if I risked my life jumping off a bridge the day before co-leading a group of nearly fifty guests. However, Wendi added, "This would be at your own expense."

Not unlike Peru, Wendi had planted the seed, and I wanted to run with it. But I felt tentative because of my neck injury. I clearly didn't want to reinjure myself, so I sought permission and called my neurosurgeon's office in New York. Because Dr. Z was unavailable, I explained my question to the office manager who said he would call me back with the doctor's recommendation.

The following morning, I received a call from an 845 area code. It was Dr. Z's office manager saying, "Dr. Z says your neck is fully fused and as healthy as anyone else's. You can jump off a bridge, but he doesn't understand why you would *want* to do it."

I thanked her. My decision was made. I would jump.

All the arrangements were easily made: go online, enter credit card number, done. However, the mental game up to that day proved difficult. T minus x days until jump! Am I sure I want to do this? T minus y days until jump! I'm going to do this. Tic toc tic toc.

Meanwhile, Eve and I talked on the phone weekly to iron out special events, dinners, costume parties, and more. In preparation for this monster of tours, we knew we would have to divide and conquer. But once we were in Auckland, a day before the group, the daunting task loomed large. She commented, "I don't know about you, but I'm kinda nervous about your jump tomorrow. Aren't you?" I laughed and took a sip of my cold Steinlager. "Of course, but I've got to do it. Some people's version of traveling to New Zealand involves wine tasting and seeing an All Blacks game. But New Zealand for me is all about adventure."

## OFF TO THE AUCKLAND BRIDGE

The next morning I met my two jump buddies, both women in their fifties originally from Puerto Rico but living in Florida. As we waited for our ride to the Auckland Bridge, we all felt nervous. Who on earth thinks jumping off a bridge is normal?

After a short drive to the base of the bridge, we locked away our purses and cameras, visited the restrooms one last time, and got suited up with an appropriate-sized harness. All set. The three of us followed our female guide to the bridge, up a set of stairs, and along guarded walkways. We each had a carabiner and strap attached to our own harness that was then attached to a cable running across the stairs and walkways to ensure no accidents.

Off we went, no turning back. No one was walking as confidently as earlier in the day. Our steps were calculated over the rushing traffic below. Even while feeling unnerved, though, we took in the amazing views of the Auckland skyline and the bay's beautiful jade-like waters.

Within ten minutes, we arrived at the jumping station where two adrenaline junkies, both cute guys from New Zealand and probably in their early twenties, welcomed us with a small disco ball and music playing. They would lighten the mood!

## SHOW AND TELL

In a playful way, one of the young Kiwis [New Zealander] walked the metal plank and, in a show-and-tell fashion, told us what to do and what NOT to do when jumping. Then he jumped head first, touching the water below and bouncing back four or five times before his partner pulled him back up to the platform. As he stood up, he looked directly at us. "Who's next?" Out of tour-director habit, I volunteered to go last, letting the others go first. However, I think this technique backfired. The longer I waited, the more jittery I got. Unlike my first skydiving jump, I didn't write my clan a letter before this adventure. They already knew. Rightfully so, my parents weren't thrilled about my doing this activity. On the other hand, Brian had encouraged me wholeheartedly.

After my two jump mates threw themselves off the bridge and successfully came back, I hobbled with the bungee tying my feet together to the platform. I said to the jumpmaster, "I will not be looking down. Just tell me how far to go and when to jump." Within seconds, I smiled hesitantly for the camera. Then I was given my clearance to plummet to my thrill-seeker pleasure. "Ready. Set. Bungee jump!!!"

OMG. In seconds, I fell toward the cold waters of the harbor. Then once the bungee had reached its max length, I bounced back almost to a vertical standing position under the bridge. I continued to bounce and bounce again until I felt the bungee pulling me back to the pod.

Hanging upside down, my nose ran as if the gates of my sinuses had flung open. That jump had literally knocked the snot out of me. To prevent more blood from going to my head as well as snot from coming out of my nose, I pulled a cord that kept me tethered to the bungee cord but allowed me to flip right-side-up to a seated position as the two Kiwis pulled me up to the jump platform. Most vividly, I recall the kick-ass view of the SkyTower and the bay. But did anyone have a Kleenex?

## WHAT A VIEW!

Although the view was impressive on the walk over, what could I say about the super-focused, adrenaline-vision post-jump view? My body, pumped full of adrenaline, shook for the next hour. I had jumped. I had triumphantly worked through the fear of it. *I had jumped.* And I knew: If I could jump off this bridge, I could tackle whatever a tour of fifty people throws my way.

| CUBA | CHPTR 30 |

# SHOULD HAVE PLAYED THE LOTTERY— INCLEMENT WEATHER

After almost three weeks with the group of fifty—other than one lost wallet, an extreme case of plantar fasciitis (inflammation of heel of foot causing soreness), a handful of seasick cases, a broken CPAP machine (to assist someone with sleep apnea during the night), a few roommate switches because of snoring, and one slip and fall with minor tailbone bruises—when considering the odds, Eve and I got away amazingly well.

Given the high probability for more trauma and drama due to sheer numbers, I felt lucky. Would my luck run out?

In Sydney, while I continued on a land tour with thirty of our guests, Eve and twenty other passengers returned to their homes in the States. I would have given anything to switch spots with Eve, for I had hit my limit. Although it is difficult to believe, I'm an introvert. Yes, I can function in entertainer mode like an extrovert while on tour and in groups. But to recharge my batteries, I prefer to be alone—as introverts do.

My group of thirty boarded a flight from Sydney to the Northern Territory and landed at a small airport outside of Uluru-Ayers Rock National Park. Although the cruise through New Zealand and Tasmania had been breathtaking, the Ayers Rock and Great Barrier Reef finale was the most highly anticipated part. They were two "bucket list" destinations for everyone, even me.

## RAIN IN THE DESERT

However, our arrival at the Ayers Rock airport was greeted with drizzle and dense cloud cover. What were the chances of traveling to the desert when it's raining? Although we didn't expect this inclemency as we got our first view of the seven-hundred-million-year-old rock, the locals were excited. For people living in a desert, rain is like winning the lottery. Many drove out to the lookout points so they could take photos of Ayers Rock draped in cascades of rainwater.

During two days at the park, we had high hopes of capturing in photos the burnt orange and red monolith with a sunset or sunrise. When would our luck turn—the next morning at sunrise? Alas, more rain. In fact, with all the rain, some portions of the resort lost power, which affected our pre-booked lunches and other activities. In spite of these conditions, though, some adventurous guests and I donned raingear and learned how to throw boomerangs.

## RAIN, RAIN GO AWAY

The rain continued into the following day, our last. That evening, our final dinner—an Outback BBQ under the stars with didgeridoo music—had to be cancelled. It was raining so hard, we expected to soon witness kangaroos lining up two by two to get on Noah's Ark.

Given the inclement weather, I knew the group's mood was grim. Despite the rain and the overall exhaustion from three weeks of travel, I wanted to make magic with the hotel staff, so we teamed up to create the Australian Outback BBQ under the stars inside the hotel. We had a didgeridoo player and complimentary wine for everyone as well as a hotel credit for gifts, meals, drinks, or services.

After two days of rare rain in the red dessert, we boarded a plane to Carnes, a seaside city and gateway to the Barrier Reef—the finale of our marathon tour. We arrived at our hotel without a hiccup but were annoyed to find it under construction. However, the upside was *no rain* predicted for the following day—our trip to the Great Barrier Reef. Little did I know we were in the calm before the storm.

## GREAT BARRIER REEF AND ITS DELIGHTS

The following day, we boarded a catamaran to a floating city on the Great Barrier Reef where we planned to spend the day snorkeling, SCUBA diving, riding submarines, and even going up in helicopters. I did it all except SCUBA diving. (I have my PADI certification that permits me to dive, but I was exhausted and short on time.)

Above all, my favorite was the helicopter ride. The reef's palette of turquoises, greens, and blues looked amazing from the air— far more beautiful than the marine life we could see near the platform. If I were a fish, I knew I'd steer clear of a floating barge of tourists—unless I was a great white looking for a snack.

## TROPICAL CYCLONE ITA

Mid-afternoon, I noticed the staff pulling furniture inside, tying down awnings, and battening down the hatches. The next thing, I heard this announcement over the loudspeaker say, "Attention passengers: the boats back to Cairns will be departing in twenty minutes. We are departing early due to an approaching tropical cyclone, Ita." Having lived in Florida for years, I had survived dozens of tropical storms and hurricanes but never while away traveling with thirty guests. I would need karma on my side.

Back at the hotel, the guests started to panic. The hotel had put out advisories. The TV news broadcast cyclone updates twenty-four seven. It looked as if the storm was heading for Queensland, and its landfall was expected the day of our departures. With most of our flights early in the morning (except mine in the late afternoon), it was predicted flights would go as scheduled. For some, though, this presented too much risk, and several changed their bookings to fly out a day early. However, the rest stayed with me for our final rainy days featuring a cancelled cable car tour due to winds, and substitute activities indoors.

Glued to the weather reports, I couldn't believe we could be stuck in the Cairns hotel because of a Down Under cyclone. I had been ready to go home after the cruise, let alone after days of rain in the desert and being stranded in Cairns. However, if we were stuck, I had to know the basics: the hotel's emergency plan, shelter, food, and most important, where the Aussies' cyclone party would be.

## DAY OF DEPARTURE

The day of departure the sea was stormy with tremendous gusts of wind and rain coming at the hotel windows in sheets. Fortunately, all the guests' flights left before noon. After calling every airline to verify if the flights were still a go, I arranged for shuttles. Everyone wanted out before the storm. No time for lengthy farewells!

With all on their way, I was all alone at the hotel by midday. I knew I could at least make it to the airport but might be held there overnight or until it re-opened. So I quickly hailed a cab. Plan A: Get out on time for a connecting flight and back to Hawaii. Plan B: Stay put until the storm passes. With my luck so far, I wasn't convinced Plan B was enough. Perhaps I needed a Plan C.

The weather gods took pity on me and Cairns that day. Tropical Cyclone Ita hit North Queensland as a category four storm. That was far enough away from Cairns to allow me to connect in Melbourne to Honolulu and then on to Kauai. After seventeen hours of flying, I was spent but safe and sound in Kauai. On the couch in our *ohana* home, I collapsed.

The previous month had been a blur. The bridge jump seemed

like a lifetime ago. Did I just survive getting out of a cyclone? If presented with this tour again, would I do it? Was this my dream job or just the opposite?

## CHPTR 31

# DAD'S CALL
# FROM FLORIDA

After my Down Under adventure in the spring of 2014, I received a call from my dad in Florida. His doctor had recommended heart surgery. When he gave me the details, he stressed it wasn't urgent but asked if I could be with him. He needed help after the surgery through recovery for about a month. Of course, I happily agreed. One of the pluses of my career was having the time and ability to write from anywhere. I booked a flight to Fort Lauderdale two weeks out.

Since leaving for New Zealand and Australia, I had approved the book cover for *When All Balls Drop*. I had also received my editor's feedback on my rough draft. She didn't sugarcoat her message; the manuscript lacked umph. She wanted more dialogue, descriptions, and clarifications on some of my Heidi-isms. I had a good month of work ahead of me, which started on my fifteen-hour, multi-leg flight back to South Florida.

However, it immediately came to a halt the day of my dad's surgery, May 20th.

## THE DAY OF SURGERY

My father and I talked that morning as we sat in his living room, both feeling apprehensive about the day ahead. He worried about the pain he'd face from the incision and wondered if he was doing the right thing. Before leaving, he pointed to the kitchen and said, "If the surgery doesn't go well, read the letter I've placed there for you."

We arrived at the Westside Regional Hospital early for paperwork, waiting, and then donning the fashionable gown and accessories of surgery—tubes for anesthesia, monitors for heart rate and breathing. Being in the cardiac ICU unit brought back many uneasy feelings of my stay in a New York hospital less than five years before. That coupled with worrying about my dad (would this be the last time I saw him?), I felt on edge. As the nurse and anesthetist wheeled him away, I said, "I love you, Dad. I'll see you shortly."

After hours of waiting in the family waiting room, one of the two surgeons came in to speak to me. Calmly and matter-of-fact, he said the surgery was complete and my father was doing well. Then he elaborated that in replacing Dad's aortic valve and doing a bypass, they saw a lot more plaque buildup than expected. I'd have to wait about a half-hour before I could see him in the ICU.

## IN THE ICU

My father was intubated when I entered the ICU. He was unable to speak and just coming out of anesthesia, so I simply held his hand and said, "I'm here." The first several check-ins by the anesthetist and nurses indicated my father was okay. His vitals were stable, and he responded to voice prompts to squeeze both of his hands and wiggle his feet. Within another hour, they predicted he'd be stable enough to remove the breathing tube. At this point, I had not updated my uncle or my friends who'd been sending text messages all day. Among the noise of beeping monitors, the breathing machine, and the inflatable calf cuffs, I could barely complete a thought.

Here's how I responded to Dad's brother via text:

*H: out of surgery still intubated but ok*

It was that afternoon, perhaps an hour after that text, when our world changed.

The anesthetist came in. He asked my father to squeeze his right hand and then his left hand. He followed suit with my father's feet. My dad couldn't move his right hand or foot. When he tried to say something, he couldn't with the tube in the way. Then he moved his left hand to point to his right arm. What was he trying to communicate to me? I could see in my father's eyes that he was scared.

## STROKE ALERT

Then I heard over the intercom, "Stroke Alert." Instantly, two nurses and the anesthetist unhooked the machines to transport him for a stroke scan. I held my father's left hand and looked at him. "Dad, they're going to do some scans and bring you right back. I'll be here."

With only the cacophony of ICU sounds to keep me company, I texted both my uncle and Brian:

H: *he can't move his right side*

The next thing I knew, the nurses wheeled him back in, various doctors came and went, several nurses grabbed clipboards, and finally the second surgeon came in. He ordered another scan as the first scan showed no signs of a stroke, so my father was wheeled away once again. I called Brian sniffling, tears streaming down my face. "My dad can't move his right side. I think he had a stroke."

Not knowing how to respond, he tried by saying, "I'm sorry. I wish I could be there with you."

"The doctors won't say anything because the scans don't prove a stroke. However, I beg to differ. If it walks like a duck, quacks like a duck, it's a duck. It was a stroke."

Although I just wanted to cry, I heard the ICU doors opening, and the sounds of the nurses and bed coming down the hall. I hung up the phone, then I blew my nose and wiped my eyes to appear less of a mess. With love in my heart, I smiled at my dad and touched his hand.

Because of the chance of another stroke, they needed to leave the tube in until the following day. The ICU nurse said, "Heidi, go home for the night. You can come back as early as you want. I'll be here taking care of him until eight in the morning."

My dad was already in and out of sleep with the pain medications. I spoke softly to him and he opened his eyes, "I'm going home. I'll be back here first thing in the morning."

## THE LETTER

After leaving the ICU and hospital, I let go. With an endless stream of tears, I drove back in his car to our home, which smelled like him. I went to the kitchen. I hadn't eaten much of anything that day, but I wasn't hungry. Even though I knew I should eat, I didn't. I would typically pour a glass of wine, but that didn't appeal to me at all.

Then I saw the envelope he left for me. He intended for me to only read it if the worst happened. But the house felt empty without him in his typical rocking chair in front of the TV. So I opened it and read, "You were the love of my life."

I sat in Dad's chair and rocked.

# THREE-LEGGED BAR STOOL

Life certainly threw my dad a shitball sandwich. A healthy, active seventy-eight-year-old man who sported a thong at the beach had been leveled by a little piece of plaque.

The day after surgery, Dad's cardiologist confirmed it indeed had been a stroke. Not a novice to the incompetence of the healthcare system, I asked him to speak to me in private outside of my dad's room. "I want to know who is the foreman of my dad's health? I've already talked to both of the surgeons and now you. If we need something, where does the buck stop?"

In a highly domineering way, he said, "I'm the lead doctor. I suggest you start planning."

"Planning? My dad is in the ICU. Just minutes ago, you confirmed our own diagnosis of stroke. What do you mean?"

"As an only child, you may want to move back from Hawaii. In the next day or so, you must find a rehab center. The sooner he starts rehab, the better the chances of regaining his movement and improving his speech."

I asked him for recommendations for rehab in the area, which he gave me, along with uninvited suggestions for two assisted living facilities. It was as if he was already writing off my dad's recovery. I said firmly, "Plan A is full recovery. Plan B is living a different life, but in his own home with my help or aids."

## DAD'S BIGGEST CHALLENGE

In the role of daughter, healthcare advocate, and bulldog, I returned to my dad's room. Thankfully, he was still in and out of sleep with the pain medications. I knew him. This would be his biggest challenge—to work to regain his speech, mobility, and ultimately his independence. My experience of losing everything and *in particular* my health taught me numerous lessons of how to maneuver in the healthcare industry. I also learned how perspective, humor, and a clan's support can get us through it.

His world wasn't the only life that changed that day. I found myself on my wonky three-legged bar stool again. Those same legs of health, love, and career that were all lost in the fall of 2009 had regrown into a stable place. I was healthy. I was in love again. I had a DIY career with tours and writing. However, my three-legged bar stool of life had tilted once again.

**CHPTR 33**

# MONTHS OFF THE ROAD AND PLAN B

That summer, because of my career choice, I took the opportunity to stay in Florida and help my father. With no tours scheduled, I dedicated the summer to editing and submitting the final copy to my book publisher for a September due date.

However, I hadn't planned on staying in Florida more than a month. One month turned into three, during which time I found my father a rehab center, stayed with him every day, and got his home ready for his return. When he went to his physical and occupational therapy sessions, I would write while in his room. In effect, my desk was his hospital table. Witnessing my father's experience, I was transported back to specific milestones in my recovery: release from the hospital, bittersweet homecoming, removal of my immobilization brace, and more.

## DAD'S RECOVERY

After his doctor's clearance, I brought my father home slightly more than a month after his surgery date. His leg mobility began to come back little by little through physical therapy. At that time, his walking was labored and shaky even with a quad cane. However, his right arm had little to no movement. As he exited the rehab center, I played the theme song from "Rocky" on my iPhone. The music matched the Superman T-shirt I'd gifted him in rehab as well as the Superman duct tape decorating his cane.

Once at home, he was feeling the same mixed emotions I did after going back and seeing my surroundings with new eyes. Yes, it was still his house with his collection of nude art and tiki bar in the living room, but *he* had changed.

Also, some of the house had changed. In preparation for his return, I had paid contractors to add shower rails and adjustments for the commode. And I ordered a box spring to place under his futon mattress so his bed would be elevated. With these additions, he would get closer to living independently with help: mine, aids, friends, and family.

We had made it to Plan B.

# *LA DOLCE VITA* — RETURN TO THE ROAD

That fall I returned to touring—not to Cuba but to Italy. Getting ready to leave, I felt anxious. Foremost, I felt apprehensive leaving my father. It would be his first week alone. However, I was also nervous about the tour. The last time I had been to Italy I was in college. The Roman ruins hadn't changed since then, but I would visit the Eternal City differently—this time as a guide to thirty mostly baby boomer guests.

In between book signings for my debut book and opportunities to do presentations, I studied Italian while driving in the car. I even spent time on the stair climber at the gym listening to and repeating Italian phrases. In the evenings sitting next to my dad in his rocking chair, I researched restaurants, museums, shopping, and historical facts about the places on the tour, especially in those cities completely new to me: Florence, Siena, and San Gimignano.

Granted, as the tour director and not the local guide, I wasn't supposed to be the bearer of all local information, language, demographics, customs, recipes, holidays, and the like. A local guide would accompany us. However, whether during those local tours or in the middle of the night, I was the twenty-four/seven problem solver. If someone was sick, not getting along with a roommate, had accommodation issues, or lost a wallet, I was "on" at all hours.

Still, going to Italy gave me a dose of *La Dolce Vita* (The Sweet Life). It allowed me to remove myself from the situation, focus on something new, and gain a fresh perspective. Plan B would become the new normal. To ease my worries about Dad, my uncle and aunt came from Missouri to South Florida to stay a few days with him. For the remainder of my absence, we agreed he would email each day to let me know he was okay.

## CUBA | CHPTR 35

# A SURPRISING SECRET

That fall I received an email from Yislaine—a complete surprise. Since we hugged at the Havana airport a year earlier, a lot of water had gone over the dam and under the bridge. In that email, she shared her secret—she was in Texas with her boyfriend, Javier, who was living with family in the Houston area.

Although Cuban immigration to the States tends to focus on Florida, the risks involved in rafting from Cuba across the Florida Straits are high. So another way for Cubans to enter the U.S., with the same "wet foot, dry foot policy", is through a third country, the most popular being Mexico. I suspected Mexico was the route Yislaine took.

A little more than a week passed after her email. Then as I was in the Dallas airport flying to Kauai to visit Brian for my birthday, my phone rang. Although I didn't recognize the number, I answered. It was Yislaine. Like an excited high school girl, I yelled, "I can't believe it's really you. You are *here*. Are you okay? How are things in Houston?"

She answered, "I can't believe it either. I arrived in September. It was so hard. I went through Mexico. Getting to the border was difficult. Even at the border, I waited for two days with little food and water. But I made it."

"Where are you living?"

"Javier came months before me. He and I are staying with his aunt and uncle in Houston. I'm working at a Cuban restaurant now. I'm even planning on getting a car."

"Wow. This is terrific news. I'm so happy for you. What's your address? I want to send you a copy of my book. Did you know the same month that you arrived, I released my book?" She congratulated me and told me her address as my flight began to board.

Yea. My sister from another mister was embarking on her Life 2.0 in Texas.

| CUBA | **CHPTR 36** |

# EARLY NEW YEAR'S RESOLUTION— BOOK 2

That fall after returning to life on the road with the tour to Italy, I started another type of tour: book signings at bookstores in Miami, Boston, and Kauai. Then I expanded this tour to include unique settings such as a local vineyard near my hometown of Galesville, Wisconsin. This allowed me to mix work with pleasure, including revisiting favorite stomping grounds, friends, and family. Like life as a tour director, this book tour required a lot of different beds, rental cars, and layovers.

Inevitably the same question came up at all of my book signings and even in conversations with my clan: "What's next?" I had left readers of my first book at a page-turning moment about embarking on a new life. What happened next? Where is she now? Although my friends and family knew my story first-hand, they also wondered what was on the horizon.

So well before New Year's, I made yet another resolution. I'd write my second book, *With New Eyes*, and release it exactly one year after my debut book *When All Balls Drop*. Fortunately, I had no tours planned until late spring when I would guide a cruise through the Hawaiian Islands. That December, I started by rereading my journals from the summer of 2010 to early 2011 when I did my solo walkabout in South America. This sparked the writing process. Before the New Year, I had nearly seventy vignettes completed—the fastest writing I had done yet!

## CUBA CALLS AGAIN

On December 14, 2014, I stopped writing as I saw the news unfolding: U.S. and Cuba had announced the reestablishment of diplomatic relationships. Although it wouldn't affect trade and the U.S. embargo, it would mean that embassies would be reopened in both U.S. and Cuba. With more diplomacy other changes were predicted to unfold *poco a poco*. Only a few days after the historic announcement between Presidents Raul Castro and Barack Obama, I received a call from Jacqui's boss, Hank. He started, "Hey, Heidi. Long time no talk. Jacqui tells me you are in Hawaii writing."

"That's right. Aloha to you. How are things?"

"That's why I'm calling you. I need a favor. One of our tour managers had an emergency. We have two tours, one in January and the other in February, that are fully booked, but we don't have a tour manager."

Just as everything about Cuba was hot and getting hotter, my old job was calling in a favor. It was very last minute. I knew they couldn't run the tours legally without a tour director. However, I didn't say a thing in the moment out of sheer amazement.

Hank continued, "It would take a lot to bring someone up to speed in time, and you already know the tour backwards and forwards. Would you be available to guide one or both of these tours?"

"Hank, give me the dates again. I'd need to think about it overnight after speaking to Brian and my father. If I'm able to swing it, I'd need to change plane tickets as well as reschedule some events," I told him.

He said that was fine. Jacqui was no longer heading the Cuba tours but another operations manager, Liz, would be emailing me with all of the details.

"Thank you for considering it. Let Liz and me know. And congrats on the book, by the way."

I didn't need to look up dates; I knew I was available. Coincidentally, I had purchased a plane ticket in January to Fort Lauderdale to help my father and speak at an event. After that, I had planned to return to Kauai to continue editing my second book for the weeks up to my Hawaii tour.

But Cuba called. I said yes, delighted I'd be surprising my Cuban friends in January.

# HIGH ALERT ON THE UNFRIENDLY SKIES

*"Every occasion in life is either a good time or a good story."*
– Unknown

This truth certainly applied to our deluge in the desert Down Under as well as a close call with Cyclone Ita—not good times but definitely good stories. Let me share another tale about an eventful return flight to Fort Lauderdale from Kauai. It's definitely a good story that debunks the phrase "the friendly skies."

On most flights, there's nothing great to write about: tight space, bad food, and the ever-shrinking legroom and tray tables. One flight in particular was a total of fifteen hours over three legs of travel with arrival in Fort Lauderdale the following afternoon. I predicted it would be a test of my endurance and patience.

With that said, I was prepared for the voyage: well fed, a couple glasses of wine, and drafted manuscript ready to edit en route. After a sad, tearful goodbye to my PIC, I boarded the plane, crossing my fingers that I wouldn't have to check my backpack because I was in the last boarding group. People in all the other groups—elite, preferred, select, gold, and silver—had gone ahead of me, taking every available overhead compartment. Still, this flight started well. The middle seat between my aisle seat and my seatmate's by the window was free. Plus, I was able to finagle my backpack into an overhead compartment two rows behind me. The first six hours would go by like a breeze—or so I thought.

## ABRUPT AWAKENING

After takeoff, I quickly drifted off. An hour later, I was abruptly awakened by a confrontation behind me between a female passenger and a female flight attendant. Groggy, I didn't turn around until the yelling escalated and the head flight attendant ran by me, bumping my seat and knocking my not-so-funny bone. Ouch!

A late-forties Caucasian woman, the mother of three young boys ranging from eight to twelve, was the passenger in question. Although I had noticed her, her three boys, and her aging mother as they boarded, I thought her being disheveled was due to holding together a multigenerational trip. Apparently, she (Winnie the Wino or WW) had mixed a little too much booze and who knows what else to prompt what happened next.

Apparently before I awoke, WW physically disciplined her eldest son who was teasing one of his younger brothers. The grandma thought the smack was too aggressive, prompting the first flight attendant to come closer. Not taking parenting advice from anyone, WW immediately went on offense with the flight attendant, swearing at her for judging her parenting. Before long, she assaulted the flight attendant by pushing her in the aisle, prompting the other head flight attendant to rush in to help (and hit my funny bone on the way).

## TURNED UP THE VOLUME

With more attention and accusations from both flight attendants, WW turned up the volume, began to kick, and threatened to sue the airline. This put me on high alert. I wanted this crazy woman tied down. Where were the air marshals? Could we sedate her?

With permission from the captain, the head flight attendant pulled out of her pocket a heavy-duty set of zip ties to restrain WW in her seat. The sight of the zip-tie cuffs threw her into a frenzied fight, kicking more, flailing her arms wildly, and screaming almost animal-like. Two men seated behind WW immediately stood up. They were both close to two hundred pounds and beefy like bodybuilders. They forcibly held WW's arms down as the head flight attendant secured the cuffs.

## WISHFUL THINKING

After that in-flight entertainment, I turned around feeling the problem at hand was solved. Wishful thinking. Although WW was restrained, she wailed in pain or shouted accusations at her boys, mother, and the flight attendants for the remainder of the flight. I give her credit for endurance. This obviously wasn't her first fight. And she continued for nearly five more hours.

In passing, I overheard that the captain had decided to continue to Phoenix instead of making an emergency landing in Los Angeles to allow the authorities to arrest WW. I was thankful for not adding any more hiccups to my already inconvenient, lengthy, and eventful journey. However, upon landing, this experience was not over. The police boarded the plane and took WW away in official cuffs, with her mother and three sons trailing. Then another crew of officials boarded the plane asking for witnesses. It was nearly twenty minutes after landing that I could grab my things and deplane, rushing to catch my connection.

## BACK TO THE NORMAL CRAZINESS

Fortunately, I made my second flight, slept awhile, and even began to proofread my manuscript. My third and final leg was uneventful as well. But that flight to Florida from Hawaii certainly shifted my perspective. I was grateful to get back to the "normal" craziness of airports and flying the unfriendly skies. Bring on the cramped seats, no snacks, and carry-on fees. At least, there was no Winnie Wino on my other flights.

As a seasoned traveler, I never leave home without my iPhone, peanuts, and a sarong. Since this eventful flight, I have added zip ties to my list.

## CHPTR 38

# HOMECOMING TO CUBA

I was anxious but also eager to return to Cuba. Was all the hype true? Was change happening fast in Cuba since the December 14th announcement?

When I met my group of twenty in Miami, I fell right into the routine and Cuba 101 info: cash only, bottled water, two currencies, hotel expectations, typical restaurants, and safety. Of course, I set up everyone with a *compay*—a buddy. I didn't want to lose track of a guest on my homecoming trip!

Ironically, everyone on the guest list for this Cuba trip came from the Midwest—as if someone handpicked the list for me. In fact, one of the couples lived in La Crosse, Wisconsin, and the wife graduated from my small high school, G-E-T High in Galesville. Yes, I went to G-E-T High. Ha ha! I've heard it a thousand times.

Over the next week, I visited my Cuban friends and left with a "mule" list for my return trip in February. I also confirmed my gut instinct—that little change had happened in Cuba. The announcement by the heads of state was just a show. For example, as on other trips, we had no water at the hotel the first day in Cienfuegos. But this time, we were competing with a cruise ship full of European tourists. Not a typical five-thousand-passenger ship, this one had about five hundred passengers. Still, the presence of cruise ships was damaging the town. Tourism from all around the globe had increased, leading to a fear of an eminent U.S. investment invasion. Everyone wanted to see Cuba before it changed. No one wanted to wait to see Old Havana with Starbucks and McDonald's. Travelers were afraid that what has happened to other destinations would happen in Cuba. It would become Americanized and quickly.

## THE NACIONAL HOTEL

As a treat (or so I thought), this trip marked my first time staying in the iconic Nacional Hotel with a group. Over the decades, it has welcomed world-renowned actors, musicians, politicians, and even mobsters. To see the wonders that have graced the Nacional's halls since it construction in 1930, just visit its Hall of Fame Bar.

First off, the check-in process was a fiasco. Not only was the lobby and property as busy as a beehive, every guestroom had a problem. While one room had no electricity, another had an overflowing toilet. Reception tried to put two solo travelers in a one-bed room—the start of a game of musical rooms instead of musical chairs. In this particular case, the room situation for one couple wasn't resolved, so I offered my room. (That's why I never unpack my suitcases after I check in.) On some occasions, this gesture requires me to stay at another hotel but not this time. At this Havana landmark hotel, I got a musty room with no view and a finicky toilet that flushed every third time.

The increased tourism due to the hype of improved U.S./Cuba relations had another effect. Customarily, I bring tips for our hotel staff, guides, drivers, and restaurant servers. They'd receive them after services were rendered. On this trip, instead of waiting for the tip envelope, staff members were asking for it almost before their service was provided. When this occurred more than once, it left a bad taste in my mouth. Change had arrived and so had greed. I had hoped for positive change to help the Cuban public. What I witnessed was more tourists being serviced with the same number of hotels, buses, and roads. Increased greed meant decreased service quality in hotels and restaurants. *No me gusta!*

## CHPTR 39

# CUBAN CUISINE 101–MOROS Y CRISTIANOS

It is no secret people learn a lot about a culture through food. That's why I try everything at least once when I travel. Also, I like to snag one or two recipes. You have already learned how to make mojitos, *cancháncharas*, and the heavenly coconut natilla.

However, no Cuban experience or meal would be complete without beans and rice. It's a staple. As my Cuban friends joke, you have a choice between rice and beans or beans and rice.

Unlike *frijoles* (beans) in Mexico, Cuba's most typical side dish is called *moros y cristianos* (The Moors and the Christians), which is a mixture heavy on the rice and light on the beans. Using the water from the beans to cook the rice, *moros y cristianos* take on a black, dirty color. Many would compare this to dirty rice from the southern States, or even *arroz congri*\*\* from some of the other Caribbean Islands.

\*\*This dish has many nicknames: moros, congri, or arroz moro

## RECIPE FOR *MOROS Y CRISTIANOS*

Ingredients:

- 2 cups white rice (*arroz*)
- 2 cups black beans (*frijoles*)
- 4 tbsp. cooking oil (*aceite*)
- ¼ lb. ham diced (*jamón*)
- 2 medium onions diced (*cebolla*)
- 1 medium sweet red pepper diced (*pimiento rojo*)
- 1 medium green pepper diced (*pimiento verde*)
- 4 tbsp. dry white wine (*vino blanco*)
- 4–5 garlic cloves (*ajo*)
- 8–10 sprigs basil (*albahaca*)
- Water (some from cooking the beans) (*agua*)
- Salt (*sal*)

Equipment:

- Rice cooker (*olla arrocera*)
- Cutting board (*tabla para cortar*)
- Knife (*cuchillo*)
- Large slotted spoon (*cuchara calada*)

Preparation Time: 30 Minutes

Instructions:

1. Dice all onions, peppers, and ham into rough cubes.
2. Smash the garlic and leave the skins on the cloves to add more Cuban *sabor* (flavor).
3. Add oil to the hot rice cooker.
4. Add the vegetables, ham, and garlic to the rice cooker and sauté while stirring with the slotted spoon.
5. Add the dry white wine and stir.
6. Add the rice and beans in their own broth and stir.
7. Peel the basil sprigs and place the full leaves in the rice cooker and stir in 1 cup of salted water (**Rule of thumb is to flavor the water/broth to the same flavor as salt water of the ocean. Add salt to the cup of water and taste. Remember to do the same to the black beans and its broth as well.)
8. Let the mixture cook for 30 minutes until the rice is fully cooked.

Serve as a side dish for other Cuban cuisine favorites such as roasted pork or *roja vieja* (shredded beef dish).

As would be typical in Cuba, be sure to say, *"Buen provecho"* (Enjoy your meal)!

## CHPTR 40

# BUEN PROVECHO! (ENJOY THE MEAL!)

When I started traveling, peanuts were served on every flight. As a peanut addict, I was hooked on plane travel for that alone. Over the years, the peanuts have all but disappeared, going the way of the smoking sections. I completely agree with removal of the smoking section. (What in the world were airlines thinking by allowing smoking in the first place within a confined, closed space?) However, going back to peanuts, I believe that dietary restrictions and some allergies have gotten out of control. Why ban all peanuts from flights? I certainly would understand if a passenger or an attendant has an allergy, but where does it end? Someone's allergic to pretzels, another person doesn't eat cookies, and there's always someone who doesn't eat anything packaged in plastic.

## EATING HABITS

Along this journey as a serial traveler as well as tour manager, the world of food has changed. So have my eating habits. I started my travels in Puerto Vallarta, Mexico, with my parents at the age of ten. At that time, I ate only fruit plates, sherbet, and French toast. I was not an adventurous eater, to say the least.

It all changed when I worked at my hometown restaurant, then moved to college and eventually landed in Madrid, Spain, for two years. Because of Spain's tapas, I became a "why not?" kind of eater. Luckily, I've never had a food allergy. My allergies are related to insect bites: bees, hornets, wasps, and more. (Oh, I'm also allergic to cubicles!) Nor have I opted to become dairy-free. I think my maternal grandfather, a cheesemaker in Mindoro, Wisconsin, would turn over in his grave if he knew I gave up cheese.

In fact, I eat meat, chicken, fish, tofu, soy, and just about everything else. I even tolerate some raw fish, but please don't expect me to go wild for a sushi bonanza. Nothing makes my stomach turn more than an extra-large piece of raw whatchamadinger served on a sticky rice nugget, no matter how much ginger, wasabi, or soy you put on it. To this day, I thank whoever created the extra-large bottles of Sapporo and put side dishes such as edamame and seaweed salad on the sushi menu. With that said, I wouldn't refuse to eat sushi or ask a chef to prepare something else at a sushi restaurant or anywhere else.

## SPECIAL REQUESTS HAVE MULTIPLIED

In my role as tour manager, I receive notification of my guests' names, ages, room assignments, celebrations, and special requests—in particular, allergies, medications, or dietary restrictions. When I started doing this, commonly only one person would be allergic to shellfish and then perhaps a token vegetarian.

However, over the years, the manifests with special requests have morphed into at least a third of the guests having a special diet: pescatarian, vegetarian, vegan, gluten-free, lactose-intolerant, Kosher, raw, or smoothies only. When my tours with large groups were on cruise ships, these requests were a piece of cake. But the more rural, remote, and off-the-beaten path we were, the less likely we'd have a lot of options. Above all, in Cuba the menus are pretty standard—always P, P, or P—pork *(puerco)*, chicken *(pollo)*, or fish *(pescado)*. The side dishes typically include cooked squash and *moros*, which may or may not contain animal fat for cooking. In many cases, an omelet is the only vegetarian option. By the end of an eight-day trip of eating an omelet for breakfast, lunch, and dinner, I thought many guests would have switched back to eating meat. I certainly would have switched because eight days of omelets means twenty-four meals of eggs, eggs, and yes more eggs. No thanks! What else have you got?

As a norm, once I met each group, I'd ask for two major things: notify me of all allergies or medical issues to be aware of and tell me any dietary restrictions. On average, a handful of guests would notify me about their details. For example, on one trip I had four kosher guests, but how kosher did they need to be? After all, we were headed to the land where the national dish is roasted pork. So over the eight-day tour, I called in advance to each of the nearly two-dozen restaurants to learn if the soup, beans, or other menu items had pork. In instances like this, aside from the main group, I recommended that the guests in question bring along gluten-free, kosher, or other types of appropriate snacks. I reminded them that there wouldn't be a Whole Foods or convenience store until they got back to the States.

## CHANGING THEIR TUNE

Inevitably along a tour with a group, some who don't have dietary restrictions see others getting a vegetarian omelet and prefer that instead of other options. Somewhere around mid-trip, guests would change their tune about being vegetarian, vegan, or pescatarian. I've witnessed it so many times, I've learned to just roll with it. Large hotels, restaurants in developed countries, and cruise ships can accommodate dietary changes but not in Cuban kitchens. The kitchen may not have half a dozen eggs to spare—or any eggs at all. Nothing about roasted pork, *moros*, yucca, squash, and candied fruit and cheese for dessert requires eggs.

As the last person to sit down for any meal with the group, I don't eat much. Typically, I need to solve a problem, escort someone to the bathroom, talk to the chef about dietary restrictions, or arrange a birthday song with the musicians. In most cases, I don't mind. After numerous visits to the same restaurants with the same P, P, or P menu, I can skip it. But don't worry. I always have a stash of peanuts in my purse and backpack. *Buen provecho*!

## CHPTR 41

# COMMUTE WENT FROM EASY TO HARD

My commute to my Cubicle Land job had been an easy, breezy fifteen minutes. However, when I switched gears, my commute got slightly longer. It would take about forty-five minutes to get to Cuba on a direct flight from Miami. When I moved to Hawaii, no longer would a forty-five minute commute be doable. I had to fly nine hours from Hawaii to New Zealand. Many times I commuted fifteen hours to return to South Florida, only to rest up and head out for a six- to eight-hour flight to Spain, Italy, or Greece. It was physically grueling to travel so far, feel jet-lagged, and then meet a bus full of strangers expecting a competent, bubbly tour director. I should have been nominated for an Oscar for my performances straight off the plane! To rejuvenate, I make it a point to jump into the new time zone by taking a run around the town I'm in. The resulting adrenaline combined with enough caffeine is my secret.

However, leading Hawaiian cruises gave me another opportunity for an easy commute. I would fly only forty-five minutes from Kauai to Honolulu to meet about twenty guests for a cruise to Maui, Big Island, Kauai, and back to Oahu. Considering the arduous commutes of other tours, in combination with the lack of phone service and need for different currencies, touring the Hawaiian Islands was a cakewalk.

Hiccups do happen, such as one guest making a pass at me in the hot tub. I politely ignored it, but if he, a conservative, politician, would have known I was a liberal, he probably wouldn't have even gotten in the Jacuzzi. Having inside knowledge of each island's excursions and activities close to port, counting on cell phone service every day, and not having jet lag made the job pleasant. Plus, we were in port each day where I could get an Internet connection without needing to use the abysmal and costly service aboard the ship.

## SEEING WITH NEW EYES

Although I had previously visited all of the islands, I saw them with new eyes from the vantage of a cruise ship. Arriving at a town *anywhere* with a couple thousand people changes its ambiance. With that said, the highlight for me was arriving at Nawiliwili Harbor in Kauai. Although our *ohana* house was only ten minutes away, I wouldn't have time to stop in on this trip. But I would see Brian.

As an excursion choice for this cruise, Wendi and I had selected an hour-long helicopter tour with Brian's employer. When I escorted my four guests to the office, the staff surprised me with a ride-along. I would be able to fly as a passenger with my guests, but better yet I'd see Brian, our pilot. Although I'd flown with him before in Florida, Alaska, and Kauai, this was special. Our professional worlds were colliding and somewhat making sense.

For the finale of the cruise, the ship passed the Na Pali Coast of Kauai's North Shore before heading back to Honolulu. I organized a group photo and happy hour on the observation deck. From there, we could take in the eighteen miles of powerful blue Pacific waters at the feet of a majestic coastline while taking in views of steeple-like mountains and deep, lush valleys. Although I had previously hiked a portion of this coastline as well as kayaked the entire stretch, I finally understood the magnitude of the Na Pali Coast viewed from the deck of this massive ship. I shared with my guests that the week after I turned in my second manuscript to the book publisher, I would hike the twenty-two-mile round trip of the Kalalau Trail along this coast. The adventure would not be for the faint of heart.

# ADVENTURE IS MY MEDITATION

After six months of writing and editing in between two unplanned trips to Cuba and the Hawaiian Island cruise, I turned in my manuscript *With New Eyes* for publishing. Because "Adventure is My Meditation" as I say in the book, I was determined to walk my talk and celebrate with a challenging adventure—hiking the Kalalau Trail with my PIC and three others. We joined forces for a hike to remember.

We set out from the end of the road on the North Shore of Kauai near Ke'e Beach. The first six miles of the trail I had previously hiked but not the entire twenty-two-mile round trip nor with a backpack of nearly thirty pounds. With the temperature about eighty degrees and no rain forecast, we planned a three-day hike—that is, go the full eleven miles on day one, rest on day two, and return on day three.

The Kalalau Trail is the only access to the world-renowned Na Pali Coast, but it isn't for the average hiker. You must be in good physical condition. You must have quality lightweight gear. You must have low anxiety to ledges or heights and good problem-solving skills. Kalalau is no joke. It goes up and down, traversing five different valleys before arriving at the pot of gold—Kalalau Beach. To add to the danger, the trail is not well maintained. In dry conditions, the red dirt and rock cause slides. In wet conditions, the red mud gets slick and slippery. It's like ice-skating up and down precarious hills for eleven miles.

## CRAWLER'S LEDGE

I had not done the entire Kalalau trail previously because of an area called Crawler's Ledge. Although I knew the hike would be physically challenging, the bigger feat would be negotiating this uneven, narrow ledge between miles seven and eight with a pack. Once we arrived at this section, I stood and examined the foot-and-a-half-wide trail on the face of a cliff overlooking the Pacific Ocean below. Scary. I've jumped out of planes and bungee jumped off bridges, but I could always count on a chute or cord. On Crawler's Ledge, there was nothing.

I wasn't turning back, so I first talked myself through each slow step of this ledge. Carrying my pack, I questioned my ability to balance. More than half way across, I came to a large rock in the middle of the ledge—one that I'd need to step over or work around. I evaluated my options and then yelled to my PIC behind me, "Hey, you've done this before. Can you go first and help me with this pack?" Calmly, Brian the mountain goat said, "Coming." In a flash, he passed, came back, and took my pack. Then I slowly continued to step forward on the remaining ledge.

Once I arrived at a safe point, I sat against my pack, took out my water, and drank it. My heart pounded from my chest into my throat as sweat ran down every part of my body. Slowly I returned to normal breathing as I watched the others cross the ledge, go around the rock obstacle, and safely reach our side.

## LAST MILES WERE TOUGHEST

After the precarious ledge, I felt relieved, expecting the rest of the trail to be easy peasy. With another three hot miles to hike, I was wrong. Just like when I ran the Boston Marathon in 2004 in similar temperatures, the last few miles were the toughest. My muscles didn't give out on that run but my joints and bones ached so much, I felt like I was running on stumps.

Similarly, the last miles of the Kalalau Trail were slow. My knees, ankles, feet, back, and more ached. Where was my oasis filled with cold water? About a mile from the beach was a river. Knowing that, thoughts of the river kept me going, albeit slowly.

## BEING MINDFUL EVERY STEP

Various times along the way out to Kalalau, I proved the worth of the statement "Adventure is my meditation." I was very much in the moment and mindful of every step on that ledge. For the remainder of the hike, I had no to-do list running through my head or any earbuds playing music. I took in and appreciated the beauty of the Na Pali Coast and its unforgettable views. Its lush, tropical cliffs jet out powerfully from the myriad of blue hues from the Pacific Ocean.

But with the beauty came mental and physical challenges. The volcanic soil, rocks, and changing conditions forced me to pay attention to where I placed each foot.

## FINALLY AN OASIS

The oasis I dreamt of eventually came in the form of a shaded riverbed and its running river. As if like a zombie, I peeled myself from my pack and walked right into the river lying down in the cold mountain water. I didn't even take off my boots.

Soothing some of my aches, I rested for a good half-hour. Brian was the first to continue the hike. I followed suit and little by little, the others did, too. Nearing late afternoon, we hiked down a baked, earthen hill called Red Hill—brutal. I tried to go faster, but my knees wouldn't take the impact. Honestly, the last half-mile nearing the beach and campsites I don't remember. My energy was zapped, and I was in a daze.

When I found Brian setting up near the waterfall, I joined him, took off my pack, and helped forage wood as he made camp. That night, despite my exhaustion and pain, I was mesmerized by the beautiful sunset and even more by the untainted night sky. After this memorable adventure, I hoped for a good night's sleep. But who was I kidding? Camping and sound sleep don't go together. What's the upside of getting little sleep? I caught the sunrise, too.

# CHPTR 43

# MY PTSD (POST-TRIP STRESS DISORDER)

Regardless of leading a five-day tour with thirty people or a three-week journey with fifty or more, if you're the tour manager, you'd better be ON.

A myriad of problems, personalities, and health scares present themselves every day (if not every hour) in a foreign country with a different language than yours, and a remote time zone from home. Faced with a plethora of fiascos, situations, and complaints, you need to prioritize like a triage doctor: Only the essentials first and the wishes later.

Being a tour manager, tour director, or group leader isn't a well-known role. I bear some knowledge of a destination and culture, but I typically turn to local guides to add site-specific information and historic details. On any tour regardless of destination, I wear these hats: logistical genius, therapist, medic, entertainer, hand-holder, translator, timer, mediator, psychic, phone operator, waitress, bartender, photographer, security guard, weather forecaster, travel agent, ambassador, furniture mover, pest controller, pack mule, accountant, and (in Cuba especially) peepee coin distributor. Now, you understand why I have a hat box!

After any trip, I experience Post-Trip Stress Disorder (PTSD). It takes my mind and body about half a week to get back to normal. No, I'm not talking about getting back into the swing of things; I mean *feeling normal*. After prolonged exposure to high stress, constant change, and endless problem solving, I'm on high alert and autopilot, although with such exhaustion, I'd imagine a pile of gravel to be a good resting spot. With that said, on the return from all but a handful of trips, I'd wake up in the middle of the night in a sleepwalking or talking state and look for my guests. Or I'd worry about why the bus wasn't outside. Or I'd start dressing to get the tour underway.

## NO TALL TALE

This is no tall tale! I've had a history of sleepwalking since childhood when I'd wake up in the late evening while my father was watching Johnny Carson on TV. He assumed I was going downstairs to the bathroom but when I didn't come up for a while, he got concerned. Shortly after, I'd come up wearing my robe after taking a shower. It was time to go to school, right? Granted, I must have stepped out of my sleepwalking state in the shower, but mostly I operated on autopilot.

On one occasion, a witness videoed a sleepwalking event after my first New Zealand and Australia adventure. I had returned to Hawaii and our humble home, my writing abode, in Lihue, Kauai. The first night, I was thoroughly exhausted from the intense trip and lengthy return flight. I'm surprised I didn't collapse when I stepped on Hawaiian soil, although I did squeeze in a shower, snacks, and wine before hitting the bed hard. But my sleepwalking and dressing commenced a little after midnight. In my head, I didn't understand why I wasn't wearing my uniform polo shirt. Unable to locate one of these shirts because they were all dirty and still in my behemoth, I quickly put on a sundress (inside out) and grabbed my clipboard with the tour's itinerary.

By this time I had awakened Brian, so he started recording me with his phone. The video showed several minutes of me wearing an inside-out sundress and shuffling through papers on the clipboard. Then suddenly I said with authority, "By the looks of these papers, this tour is over." Apparently, I returned to bed after that.

I still don't remember this incident or many others. But, my antics have been shared at the dinner table or around a bonfire with accompanying video as they poked fun at the crazy autopilot tour manager. Desk job to dream job? There are certainly perks, but I wouldn't chalk up sleepwalking as one of them.

# HEALTH SCARES ON THE ROAD

Many have commented, "You have the best job!" or "I'd love to do what you do." Those who say these things only see a few parts of the job: several months off a year, mojitos or other local libations by noon, lots of sightseeing, and an ever-changing office. First-time observers don't see the challenges of the position. Regardless of how well you do your job keeping your guests safe and knowing your subject matter, no tour manager has the magic wand for staying healthy. Yet it's the *número uno* responsibility of this job, over which none of my peers or I have control.

Having health scares in your own backyard presents challenges. Try being on the road with a large group of strangers, of whom the majority are either baby boomers or septuagenarians. Even though both the travel agency and I request the most accurate information about particular allergies or medical conditions, many choose to ignore it. This doesn't help. Most of the time, a health issue comes about suddenly, and I receive a call that someone needs me *yesterday*.

Whether dealing with urinary tract infections in Peru, seasickness on a cruise ship across the Tasman Sea, or an in-house doctor visit at the Nacional Hotel in Havana, I've had at least one health scare on every trip. Combining a change in climate, different food, and lack of sleep takes a toll on us all. People make mistakes and overextend themselves. Even accidents happen.

## BIGGEST HEALTH SCARE

My most memorable health scare happened in 2015 on a trip to Cuba. For many, Cuba is a bucket-list destination, popularized by the movie *The Bucket List* starring Jack Nicholson and Morgan Freeman. A couple from the Pacific Northwest, Robert and Mary, had just received bad news. After booking this trip, Robert was diagnosed with pancreatic cancer. Wanting to enjoy the remaining time he had, he and Mary decided to go ahead with the eight-day trip to Cuba. He'd have chemo treatment immediately after returning home. To prepare Robert for his treatment, his doctors implanted stents in his stomach to prevent further sickness or even jaundice. However, they warned him that travel would stress his immune system as well as the success of the stents. As a precaution, his doctors prescribed various antibiotics and medications in case he fell ill while traveling.

Because of the high probability of something happening as well as the grave consequences, Mary and Robert came up to me the very first evening before leaving the States to give me this information ahead of time. I commented, "Thank you. If at any point you feel the least bit abnormal, let me know. This isn't the time to be Superman, okay?"

After a few more questions and verifying that all his prescriptions were in marked bottles, I returned to my hotel room for an early departure the next day. Not being a healthcare professional, I needed to brush up on everything they had described. Google and WebMD came to the rescue. I would have limited access to Internet service for emails back to my employer, let alone medical explanations or translations, while in Cuba. Quite honestly, I didn't know what some medical terms meant in English, so how could I explain things to a doctor in Spanish? Good thing most medical terms are Latin and Spanish-Latin based.

## ROLLED WITH THE GROUP AT FIRST

At first, the trip appeared to be going swimmingly. Robert kept up with the group and rolled with the less-than-ideal situations that occur on any travel: delays, inclement weather, traffic, and peculiar personalities in the group. Both Mary and Robert knew that, in the whole scheme of things, the issues were little compared to the big elephant only the three of us knew about.

On the other hand, a select few members of our group were stuck in complaint mode. They expected nirvana in Cuba: one hundred percent personalized, acclimatized, on-time travel with a group of twenty adults. Come on! If you believe you can have all of that, let me sell you a bridge. They must understand I always shoot for Plan A, but with weather, personalities, health issues, national holidays, strikes, or other events, at times I have no choice but to put Plan B in place.

Every day I kept a keen eye on Robert, and asked Mary aside to verify. Everything was all right until halfway through the trip when we reached the Nacional Hotel in Havana. While I was eating breakfast, another guest relayed the message that Robert was very ill. In an accusatory fashion, she said, "Mary has been looking for you. Robert is sick." I immediately left to call their room. Mary answered, "Robert spiked a fever of over one hundred. We don't want to miss any of Havana, but he's too weak."

"I'll be up in a bit. I'll bring the nurse with me."

Unlike smaller hotels, the Nacional had an in-house doctor daily and a nurse twenty-four hours a day. Although being in the busiest hotel in Havana was tiresome, the perk of having medical attention in the hotel versus taking cabs to the clinics was a saving grace. With the rest of the group meeting in thirty minutes to leave for the day, I used the same pay-per-minute phone in the lobby to call my local guide, Ramón.

"Two of our guests are not coming today. I'll be staying at the hotel with them to help with the doctor."

"Okay. What do you need me to do?"

"Go with the group. I'll try to meet you by lunchtime. If I need to go to the hospital with them, I will call you. Please notify your boss about this in case we need to book an earlier flight for them."

## HOUSE CALL

I went up to the medical office where I met a middle-aged nurse dressed in an all-white uniform. I introduced myself and explained the need for a house call by the doctor regarding Robert's pre-existing condition. Because the doctor had not yet arrived, the nurse suggested she go to Robert's room to check his vitals and start the paperwork. I went in advance to prepare Robert and Mary.

When I knocked on the door of their room, Mary promptly opened it to let me in. Out of habit, she apologized for the mess inside. I replied, "Are you kidding? You should see the tornado that went through my room!" Changing subjects, I then said, "Robert, the nurse is coming up shortly to take your temperature and vitals. The doctor will be here within an hour to follow up." That's when Mary interjected, "He has already taken the antibiotics his doctors gave him. I would like to talk to his doctors before going to the hospital. They are on the West Coast."

Then the nurse knocked. I let her in, made introductions, then translated the basics to the nurse. She took Robert's temperature— one hundred and two degrees. However, his breathing and heart rate seemed normal. The nurse noted all that on her clipboard and said we should order room service for *caldo* (chicken broth). She would send the doctor up upon her arrival.

I had experienced the international clinics in Havana and Cienfuegos with previous guests. The doctors and nurses had always been knowledgeable and polite, but the surroundings weren't up to the standards Americans expect from a clinic in terms of appearance, technology, and supplies. Knowing Robert likely had the best medications already, I commented, "I don't suggest going to the hospital unless it's urgent. Let's see if we can reduce your fever here where you'll be more comfortable."

## THEIR TRAVEL HEALTHCARE INSURANCE

Like all travelers to Cuba, upon arrival at our first airport, Robert and our group had to purchase health insurance (about three dollars for every day in Cuba) or show proof via a stamp on our tickets that the travel agency had done so on our behalf. This requirement by the Cuban government for all foreign travelers ensures that its world-renowned healthcare system is not abused. The health insurance covers doctor visits at international clinics. However, it doesn't cover medications, prolonged stays, or surgeries. Most people get scared about this, but if they do have to pay for procedures, stays, and prescriptions, they are more reasonably priced than in the U.S.

After a half-hour, the doctor and nurse both came to Robert and Mary's room. The nurse certainly looked her part, but the female doctor with her grey Afro, heavy eye makeup, and a long, gaudy necklace looked like a backup singer for Tina Turner. Thank goodness she wore a white doctor's coat over her loud clothes and carried a faux-leather medical bag.

Once again, I facilitated introductions and background information. With a personality as big as her Afro, the doctor then took over. She pressed on various areas of Robert's abdomen, asking in elementary English, "Hurt, yes or no?" She reverted back to Spanish, explaining to me that, with his pre-existing condition, not much could be done. He already had scheduled treatment in the States, so it would be best to take it easy and reduce his fever

151

with an antipyretic shot (like a shot of acetaminophen).

Robert and Mary agreed. From her bag, the doctor pulled a syringe and a vial of clear liquid. She loaded the syringe and looked at Robert. "Ouch *un poquito*." Then they instructed Mary to get chicken broth and keep Robert hydrated. The doctor promised to stop by early in the afternoon. Mary and I thanked both doctor and nurse then closed the door.

After helping with phone calls to the West Coast doctors and room service, Mary agreed that with the fever subsiding, she'd feel comfortable staying in the hotel. I left them to get rest, with a plan to check in with them at noon.

## ALERTED THE AGENCY

Although I wanted to go to my room and brush my teeth (no time between breakfast and triage), first I needed to send an email to the States regarding Robert. In the lobby, I was able to use the paid Wi-Fi and quickly alerted the agency about this medical situation. Before I logged out of the system, I received a sharp reply from my supervisor, Liz, upset that I wasn't with the group! I couldn't believe I'd get reprimanded for doing the necessary. But Liz clearly stated that since the sick patient had his wife, I should have been with the group. I had to bite my tongue and respond ever so politely by saying, "The nurse and doctor here are not bilingual. I needed to translate the very complicated pre-existing condition of pancreatic cancer. Also, I helped facilitate phone calls back to the States for his wife who is beyond stressed right now. Once his fever breaks, I will taxi over to the group for lunch and the remainder of the day."

At noon, I revisited Robert and Mary. Thankfully, his fever had broken. I agreed to return in the afternoon with the doctor and suggested resting was the best thing to do. After exiting their room, I headed to the lobby to catch an old Russian Lada taxi to the private restaurant in Central Havana where the group was having lunch. Because I hadn't eaten a full breakfast, I was starving.

After addressing everyone's concerns about Robert, I sat with our guide and driver with a unique P, P, or P. Instead of *pollo, puerco,* or *pescado,* the restaurant offered pork, fish, and pizza. Sometimes when things get rough—including health scares on the road—eating pizza is perfect.

# COMMUNAL IQ OF GROUP TRAVEL

A valuable piece of wisdom about IQ stems from a theory my father shared with me when I was still in high school. At the time, I was spreading my wings by attending parties and going out with boys. Although he knew I was a smart young woman, he commented, "Regardless of your own IQ, when people group together, the communal group IQ goes down."

In general, I think his belief is correct. Whether it's the group dare or a bet over a red solo cup (aka the universal house party cup or roadie cup) that lands someone in jail (or worse in the hospital), it happens because of the group IQ effect. This goes for group travel as well.

Further explaining this IQ phenomenon about my tour guests requires highlighting a common travel ailment called "braincation." It can describe anyone who's either traveling solo or part of a group. Eventually, one's brain goes on vacation, unable to make rational decisions, follow directions, or do simple math. So what happens when a group of doctors, lawyers, professors, engineers, and IT geniuses go on "brain-cation" traveling in a foreign country?

Duh, the individual IQs are thrown out the window, giving way to a low communal IQ akin to a bunch of Homer Simpsons. This low communal IQ mixed with alcohol, jet lag, and/or sleep deprivation makes a recipe for humdingers, including lost wallets, missing visas or passports, failure to take medications, and sleeping around. All of these, of course, become my problem. Yes, even the sleeping around becomes my issue—not because of health concerns like pregnancy or STDs, but because of gossip.

Even when traveling in a group of respectable adults, it's funny how people revert back to high school with gossip, clichés, and popularity contests. From the group arise the class clown, the president, and the prom queen. Also emerging are the teacher's pet, the menace, and the stinky kid.

Test my dad's IQ theory out at your next group trip or gathering. We may be stronger in numbers, but we're not smarter.

# MY *BODEGA* ON THE BUS

After doing the same tour through Havana, Cienfuegos, Santa Clara, Trinidad, and the Bay of Pigs nearly twenty times, I became more efficient, working smarter not harder than before. I anticipated certain items and souvenirs my guests would want that weren't always available at the hotel or would take forever to purchase in the local market. In essence, I ran a *bodega* on the bus.

In most parts of the world, a *bodega* is a place where patrons purchase wine or food. In Cuba, it's also a place to purchase food but with a twist. Since 1962, Cuban *bodegas* sell staples at a subsidized rate of nearly twenty percent less than the free market. Let me explain.

Every family receives a *libreta* (small rationing book) at the beginning of each calendar year, and it features one page a month. Each month, the family (depending on number of members and ages) receives a certain ration of rice, beans, sugar, milk, eggs, oil, and other staples. Using the *libreta*, any family member can visit his/her neighborhood *bodega* for basic purchases.

However, at times, certain staples aren't available because of shortages across the country caused by low production or no shipments. Even when all products are available, these rations only scratch the surface of what's needed to survive. So to feed a family, the rationing book is complemented by purchasing food in CUP (National Cuban Pesos) at higher prices than in the free markets. For the privileged few who have access to CUCs (Convertible Cuban Pesos, aka the tourist money), they can purchase imported goods—everything from wines and oils to personal hygiene products—in a dollar store. Unlike the American connotation of dollar stores, CUC stores in Cuba got this name because the CUC was instilled to be used instead of the U.S. dollar. Dollars stores in Cuba are by no means cheap—just the opposite.

Although I called myself "Heidi the *bodeguera*" (store owner), I was running a CUC store with stamps for postcards, Internet cards, Havana Club cocktail glasses, and pounds of Cuban coffee. Like the Cuban *bodegas*, I too would run out of highly sought-after items and most often Internet cards. Even if a Wi-Fi connection existed, at times there were no Internet cards to buy.

This also happened in 2016 when a shortage of coffee occurred.

At the largest grocery store in Havana, we found only a few bags of coffee. Why? The Carnival cruise ship had just been in town for two days picking all the shops clean.

The major benefit of my *bodega,* though, was providing change for my guests. It gave me a way to provide change in small bills, as well as peepee coins.

## UNIQUE GUEST REQUESTS

Although keeping guests safe and healthy is a large part of the job, so is making dreams come true. Over the years as tour director, I've lined up opportunities for guests to sing on stage or play guitar with the house band as well as set up a surprise caravan of a dozen old classic convertibles to tour Havana.

I have even been a matchmaker. On my first trip to New Zealand and Australia, a couple met and has since married. It just goes to show: Do what you love and love will come to you.

However, some guests' requests I simply can't complete, including niche collectables found only on eBay. On a quick tour of Havana, a female guest asked me, "Could you help me find an antique iron? I collect antique irons from all of my travels." If she would have asked for a Havana Club T-shirt, a *guayabera* (typical Cuban four-pocket shirt for men), or a set of bongos, dominoes, or earrings, I could have appeased her. But an *antique iron?* I was tempted to say, "Sure, why don't I just pull that out of my magic hat. Voila!" Instead I said, "That is a unique request. The only place to find this item might be at the book fair at the Plaza de Armas among the antiques. If you want to go there instead of the large San José Market with the group, you can walk to the Plaza from our market stop." Deep down, I knew that would be like finding a needle in a haystack.

In Cuba, the mass production of souvenirs that tourists collect, such as destination shot glasses, thimbles, or decorative spoons, hasn't taken off. Sure, you can find magnets, T-shirts, hats, postcards, and the like. With the expansion of cruise ship traffic, these items will come *poco a poco*: jewelry shops, sundries, and "safe" restaurants that serve hamburgers, nachos, and beers or mojitos in glasses as tall as you. I hope not, but the port of Havana may have a Mojitoville section before you know it!

| C U B A | CHPTR 47 |
|---------|----------|

# TWENTY QUESTIONS

A common characteristic of people working in travel or hospitality is patience. Regardless of where I lead a tour or the number of guests on it, I'd be subject to a revolving game of twenty questions requiring lots of patience. Of course, it's only natural the travelers want to know more about me or any tour manager. It's not a one-night stand; we'd spend anywhere from five days to a month together.

Guests are curious about me, viewing my life as if I were an animal in the zoo. Plus, we tour managers are a different breed. We haven't taken the safe career path with traditional benefits such as health insurance, 401(k)s, and retirement. So meal after meal as I sat with different guests, I'd answer the same questions as if pressing "play" on a recording.

## FIRST ROUND

The most common question is some variation of "How often do you lead tours?" This is followed by "So where is home?" I'd explain that I led roughly two tours a month from my Fort Lauderdale base. Then I'd add that, with Cuba in particular, I had summers off because of the intense heat as well as the Caribbean hurricane season. My off time allowed me to write as well as pick up other tour gigs around the world. Then the more adventurous would ask if I had a boyfriend or kids. Wouldn't they already know it'd be practically impossible to do my job if I were a parent?

They always wonder if I have a man in every port of call or Cuban city. No, no way. I don't mix business with pleasure, if you can call it that. Some tour directors do that, but honestly, I don't know where they find the time. On a tour, the furthest pleasure from my mind is sex because I'm worried about the other basic needs: food, water, and sleep. However, that doesn't deter guests, local tour guides, drivers, performers, bartenders, managers, and even customs officials from throwing their hats in the flirting ring. On various occasions at the Cienfuegos airport, the same customs official asked me if I was still with my boyfriend, the *piloto* (pilot). With a smile, I nodded affirmatively, after which he looked disappointed and walked me to passport control.

## SECOND ROUND

On long tours, I'd sit with guests who had already gotten the Heidi 101 lesson and were ready for more "dirt" about how I ended up as a tour director. Heidi 102 would lead me to talking about my previous careers as a Spanish teacher and then in the corporate world—until my life changed in 2009.

In fewer than thirty seconds, I'd tell my story about taking out the trash in New York and the thousand-pound tree limb that fell, breaking my neck. That tree forced my life (as I knew it then) to halt abruptly. I'd end with, "I'm fortunate. I had a second chance at life. I had a choice to rebuild my former life or be the architect of a new one, Life 2.0, and I chose the latter." Typically, sharing this would win me Brownie points as well as open an opportunity for others to talk about their obstacles. We've all had them.

## THIRD ROUND

The third round of questions comes on the final days of the tour. After the guests realize some of the challenges of my work, they ask, "Aren't you tired of seeing the same thing?" There are times (okay, *many* times) I'd like to tap my heels together like Dorothy in the *Wizard of Oz* and go home. Realistically, how many times can one see the Bay of Pigs Museum? Even the Buena Vista Social Club on my umpteenth time lost some of its charm. However, I experience the majority of the repeat places differently because of the people I'm with. I see many of the places with new eyes because of my heightened knowledge, what I'm working on, or just the way the wind blows on that particular day.

This isn't true when it comes to food, though. I can't lie. I do get sick of the P, P, or P menu. Instead, I love flavorful and even hot, spicy food. Contrary to popular belief, Cuban food is not at all spicy. Back in Miami, I'm racing to get some hot Tex-Mex, plus I put myself on a pork cleanse for a while.

## LAST ROUND

And the last round of twenty questions takes place inevitably at the farewell dinner or at the airport on the last day, as a type of validation. It's natural. There's always a part of us that wants to be accepted and liked. One of the standouts (typically the group president or the group clown) asks, "Are we your favorite group?" Even if the question comes from someone in a group who challenged me, I'd respond positively, saying, "I *love* this group. You're real good eggs."

There was one exception to this rule, when I was served a motley crew of delinquents.

# CHPTR 48

# CHARACTERS ON THE TOUR

As I said earlier, there are some travelers I *want* to lose. No, I'm not talking about the inquisitive traveler who asks question after question after another question. Nor am I referring to the on-the-prowl traveler who thinks that making passes at me, the tour manager, is fair game, despite multiple decades of difference in age. Okay, maybe I did want to duct tape the mouths of certain people and seat them at the back of the bus. But by far my top three characters had other challenges. Let me just say this: Any tour changes when substance abuse is a component. The same goes if someone isn't capable of mainstream travel because of a pre-existing mental diagnosis or disorder.

Two of my top three travel characters, Lucy Goosey and Chuck the Canuck, made the list because of their overuse and dependency on alcohol. Although I believe that enjoying wine, cocktails, and local libations is part of vacationing, playing with "functioning" alcoholics in a foreign country creates a need for caution. Without all synapses firing (aka "brain-cation"), no one needs to add the lack of inhibitions that comes with excessive drinking.

This leads to another common trait of many alcoholics, which is having no filter. More times than I can count, I have defused inappropriate comments that most adults would avoid in any social situation. Likewise, I have done the reverse to calm down an emotional reaction to something that otherwise would roll off one's back. Meet Lucy Goosey.

## LUCY GOOSEY

Lucy was a mid-fifty-year-old bottle blonde who was recently single and really liked red wine. A lot. On one particular evening, Lucy had lips stained purple from drinking wine from morning till night. Her speech was already slurred at happy hour, but she felt up to joining the group for dinner. Not knowing how to fit in at her chosen table, Lucy decided to be the know-it-all of politics and religion, both topics to avoid when trying to win friends. While sitting at another table, I eavesdropped on Lucy's group to make sure all was well. About halfway through the salad course, she let out an anti-Semitic comment toward another person. No remorse. I had no choice but to get out of my chair and approach her. Knowing I was opening a can of worms that would continue to backlash the remainder of the trip, I politely asked Lucy to speak to me away from table. She refused. Given no choice but to let everyone at the table hear, I stated, "Lucy, please remove yourself from the table. It's time to return to your cabin and sleep this off."

Steaming mad, Lucy threatened to get back at me as she left the dining room (but not forgetting to take her glass of red wine). I apologized for her behavior to the guests at her table and returned to my seat. Worried about what Lucy was getting into out of my supervision, I didn't eat a thing after my first couple bites of salad.

Although I had full authority to do what I did with Lucy, I knew the next couple of weeks would be tough. You may not be aware, but on a cruise ship, if any guest mistreats another guest or staff, the issue can be taken to the hotel director of the ship. Then it's up to the director whether to give the person a second chance or force early disembarkation at the guest's expense.

It wasn't long before the hotel director knew about Lucy. After the night she was asked to leave the table, she tried to separate herself from our group in all dining and shore excursions by calling guest relations. Of course, while calling in her inebriated state, she'd rudely demand things, and if she wasn't given exactly what she wanted, she hung up on the staff—only to call back minutes later.

Wanting to give Lucy a second chance, I called her cabin the following morning. She didn't pick up the phone, but I left a message inviting her to join the group for lunch. I also stuck a note with the same invitation on her cabin door. She was a no-show. Later in the day, I saw her in one of the hallways and called to her, "Hey, Lucy, I'd love to have you join us this afternoon and evening." She stopped and waited for me to catch up, then said, "You are a worm." She continued to her room. That evening, though, she came to dinner with a white Russian (a cocktail of Bailey's Irish cream, vodka, and Kahlua), but brought her best behavior to impress a fellow guest, Shawn.

For the remaining weeks, she continued to drink; however, Shawn's attention kept her behavior somewhat under control. Lucy would still occasionally up and leave from dinner and not come back. She also spilled drinks on another woman during our formal group picture. She only made two friends on the trip: Shawn, the one male suitor, and Chuck the Canuck.

## CHUCK THE CANUCK

Chuck was a seventy-year-old Canadian who wanted to be noticed. Every day he would sport a hat with his name in large block letters atop a large maple leaf flag with various small patches of all the other countries he had visited. Chuck had his vices. He loved to smoke and drink Budweiser, which he called Holy Water. In fact, he even had a leather holster to attach to his belt that would carry his bottle of Bud. (I thought it was quite genius, really. Remember, I'm from Wisconsin where people are known to wear beer guzzler hats to Packer games, have a dedicated beer fridge in the garage, and go on tubing trips down rivers taking an entire inner tube for the beer cooler.)

Chuck was sociable, but along with the holster and hat came the odor of half a century of cigarette smoking. It exuded from his every pore. To speak to Chuck, I had to do my SCUBA diving breathing (only through the mouth with no air through the nostrils). Other guests quickly learned of *eau d'Chuck* and picked seats away from good ole Chuck.

Unlike Lucy, Chuck never outwardly offended anyone in our group through conversation or comment; however, he did so with the cruise ship staff. One night near midnight, he became belligerent at the guest relations desk. I was not notified of

Chuck's behavior until the next day when we had a VIP group event on the helipad of the ship. There, all the officers were present. The hotel director introduced himself and then invited me to his office to discuss my group. As we walked together toward his office, he politely filled me in on Chuck's behavior as well as Lucy's calls.

"You have your hands full, but I'm here to help," he said, opening his office doors where a female officer was waiting for us. As head of guest relations, she was there to talk about the previous evening's incident. After reading the notes from the evening shift, the director had no other choice but to demand Chuck come to the office. The director explained to me he would give Chuck one more chance, but any additional occurrences would mean disembarkation. The officer said, "Just also wanted to let you know we also have notes about various rude calls and hang-ups from your guest, Ms. Lucy. They aren't as severe as Chuck's, but all staff members are aware of her hostility and drinking."

Before I left to find Chuck and ask him to head to the director's office, the officer asked me about my third character, Penny. "How is she doing after her quarantine? Does she typically travel with your company and all alone?" Let's meet Penny.

## PENNY FROM DOWN UNDER

A fifty-five-year-old blonde Australian from Queensland with autism, Penny had a rough start to the trip. As is customary, the medical staff asked all passengers about any symptoms of illness when they boarded the ship. Without much filter, Penny answered truthfully saying she'd had diarrhea the day before. Most of us would have said nothing, but Penny's answer led her to a forced twenty-four to forty-eight hour quarantine in her cabin. I was immediately notified by the ship's staff. I went to her cabin to introduce myself.

Penny was rightfully upset. I tried to calm her down, promising to do my best to get her with the group the next day. That's when I realized she would need constant guidance and clear instructions throughout the trip.

The following morning, I worked with the medical staff to okay Penny for release, and I walked her to the gangway for her shore excursion. Before she disembarked, I said, "Hey, enjoy your tour today. I'll see you back on the ship for happy hour. Remember, you'll get to meet the others. And they don't know anything about the quarantine."

At that evening's cocktail hour, Penny arrived fashionably late and ordered a Coke. Before introducing her to some of the guests, I pulled her aside and reminded her, "Hey, remember, you don't need to tell others about the quarantine. It may make some uncomfortable. Just start with where you're from and what you did today on tour." I walked with her to a group and made the introductions but was briefly pulled away by a cruise ship staff member. By the time I returned, Penny was explaining her diarrhea and quarantine to the others.

It was a rough start for Penny and probably not the best introduction, but this trip was nearly three weeks long. Thankfully, she participated in everything. Having missed out on the first day and wanting to fit in, she joined us for costume nights, scavenger hunts, and games. She even won a dice game and walked away with a jackpot, albeit a hodgepodge of American, Canadian, and other currencies.

Penny was always easy to spot. She wore her favorite rugby team's red jersey almost every day except for formal and costume nights. (We hoped she had the shirt laundered by the ship more than once.) Although she was relatively harmless, Penny's social skills and repetitive behaviors—her incessant hand rubbing and facial twitching—bothered many of the guests. I can't blame them. If I were on vacation, I wouldn't volunteer to sit next to Penny from Down Under.

Can you believe my incredible luck! All three of these characters, a definite motley crew, landed in my lap on the same multiple-week cruise. This marked my first time being called to the hotel director's office. It felt like reporting to the school principal's office. A female traveler from Wisconsin summed up the trip well by commenting, "You should be canonized as Saint Heidi for your patience."

## CHPTR 49

# CORKY'S BIG ADVENTURE

After those three characters, I needed a good dose of adventure with my PIC back in Kauai to get my wits about me. This true tale highlights that every occasion in life can be categorized as either a good time or a good story. The protagonist in this is none other than Corky, our most valuable purchase on the Garden Island.

Because much of Kauai is not accessible via road—to get up close and personal with the Garden Isle and its waterfalls —you have to go off-road via your own two feet or in a kayak. As two adventurers and PICs, we bought a used tandem sea kayak, red and orange. In its previous life, it was a rental kayak, thus showing its wear and tear. It had sun-bleached areas, rivets coming loose, and an atypical stopper—a wine cork, thus, the name Corky.

Many of our kayak adventures were pleasant day trips up gentle rivers surrounded by sea hibiscus flowers and mangroves with the green mountains as a beautiful backdrop. No wonder so many movies have been made on the island: *Jurassic Park I, II, and III; Pirates of the Caribbean; The Descendants*; and the list goes on. However, it's the misadventures that become the best stories. Who wants to hear about a sunny kayak trip downriver to a peaceful picnic without bugs? No one. That's why I share this misadventure to Kalalau.

## KAYAK RUN TO KALALAU

Our previous kayak adventure down the Na Pali Coast took effort, but the eighteen-mile kayak trip had the perfect summer conditions: three to five foot waves and mild winds. We didn't carry supplies on that trip as lunch was provided by the guide. However, our indie kayak run in Corky was a combo of kayaking and camping at Kalalau, the same secluded beach we had hiked to when we celebrated my second book.

Loaded with tents in dry bags, sleeping bags, hammocks, and a cooler with supplies for two days, Corky was heavy. To make the weight even more challenging, the seas were gnarly, six to eight foot waves with the current going with us but a fifteen-knot headwind. Needless to say, I was anxious for our safety.

Wearing my lifejacket, hat, shades, and water shoes, I jumped into the front of the kayak as we ventured beyond the beach and breaking waves. With our destination so far in the distance, I kept my eyes focused on baby steps, each valley that we passed. With the intense winds and no rudder, keeping the kayak away from the coast became challenging. As the paddler in the bow, I was in charge of the pace, but Brian's job was both power and steering. Incapable of steering myself, I'd yell back at him if I felt us getting off course, "What the hell are you doing? Steer!"

"I am, damn it. *You* try kayaking a barge."

## EYE ON THE PRIZE

After numerous breaks in bays for shelter from the wind, we headed on. With the challenging route and conditions, this was the first time I don't remember seeing marine life. Typically, I could spot sea turtles, even dolphins, but not this time. My eye was on the prize—land and Kalalau beach.

By early afternoon Brian sported another shade of sunburnt pink and both of us were salty. Then we saw the beach. A tourist catamaran had stopped in front of it for a photo op but motored away as we got closer. With aching hands and arms, a part of me wanted to jump on board the catamaran and call it a day. However, I knew once camp was set, it held a better view than any five-star resort could provide for an untainted sunset and a brilliant night sky complete with an ocean soundtrack.

## BEACHING CORKY

But my biggest challenge still lay ahead: beaching the kayak. I've learned to easily get out and in of the kayak if we capsized or I just needed to pee. But beaching has been a tough feat every time because the conditions are always different and unpredictable. In this case, I jumped off the kayak before the shore break, leaving Brian to ride the kayak to the beach. As he scrambled with the boat, I struggled swimming against a strong undertow holding onto my paddle. With the mid-afternoon sun strong and winds still intense, we both hit land glad to be out of the kayak. Thankfully, we had time to set up camp at a leisurely pace with hours before dark.

We chose to put up close to the water source where the ground was flat. I foraged firewood while Brian set up the tent. Before making dinner, we went for a walk to scope out our neighbors. Of course, we greeted the local boys' tent, typically a pair of Hawaiian brothers and their friends who help injured hikers with rides back into Hanalei via boat. They bring provisions to long-term dwellers in the valley as well as remove garbage. In Kalalau, as in a small town, it's good strategy to be friendly, so I introduced myself to the brothers. On a previous solo hike, Brian had needed the local boys' (aka pirates) assistance when he twisted his ankle. He claimed it was the best hundred-dollar Zodiac ride he's ever had.

## TIME TO RELAX

After dinner, we enjoyed the moonlight and beautiful night sky. Thoroughly exhausted, we wanted a good night's sleep. But regardless of our comfortable camping pads and pillows, we had a restless evening. Perhaps the view was better than a five-star hotel, but the sleep wasn't even as good as at a two-star, paper-thin wall, airport hotel. We got up early and had a full day in Kalalau to explore the valley, find its swimming pools, and again delight in the beautiful sunset and moonlit camping.

## PREPARING FOR LAUNCH

The following morning, we awoke to our alarm set for five o'clock. It was essential to leave early before the winds picked up in order to kayak back to our truck. The clouds were thick and the waves rough. We also knew it would be a challenge to get Corky past the breaking waves.

As we prepared for launch, the rain started. Even wearing my life vest and surfing rash guard, I was cold. At a little before six, we made our first attempt. We pushed Corky into the waves, waiting for a set of larger waves to pass and then strike for a good window of smaller waves. Standing in chest-high water, I attempted to get in, but Brian quickly said, "Get away. Get away. Abandon ship." As I scrambled away with my paddle, the waves tumbled Corky, with all our gear and cooler, into the surf.

Take two was similar, but some of the dry sacks were now taking on water, so Corky was even heavier. The sky continued to darken. The adrenaline combined with the cool rain made my body tremble. Regardless, we knew the clock was ticking. The increasing winds would only make this worse.

Brian and I set ourselves up again and waited for the right window. Then we went for it. We launched into the surf and almost past the breakers, but the waves pushed us back toward the beach once again. It was another rough tumble and spill for Corky. Luckily, neither Brian nor I had been taken along for the spill.

We didn't do a take three. I said, "We can't go out in this. Even if we both can make it past the breaking waves, it's too dangerous to keep going. We need to revert to Plan B." I took our cooler and a bag with our tent off the kayak and headed to higher ground. Upset, Brian was determined to make it out without help. At nearly seven o'clock, Brian swam Corky out to a mooring ball that was offshore. It's where the local boys tie up their Zodiac and Jet Ski.

## A BIG FAVOR

Brian and I waited to approach the pirates' tent until mid-morning when we saw their camp started to stir. We needed a big favor: two passages to Hanalei with a kayak in tow. They agreed to take us, but we needed to wait for the boat, scheduled to come around ten in the morning. But the boat's captain, Bobby, a three-hundred-pound Hawaiian man in his forties, had no intention of turning around right away. He wanted to relax, drink a bit, smoke some pot, and have lunch before returning to Hanalei. Brian and I sat and waited for our ride at the mercy of when the local boys were done "talking story" (Hawaiian creole or Pidgin way to say catching up).

Seven hours had passed from our last attempt with Corky when Pirate Bobby finally said it was time to load up. By then, a total of nine of us needed a ride into town. All the others were hikers who had over packed. They didn't want to retrace the grueling eleven-mile hike back with rainy conditions. Brian and I were the only ones with a kayak.

One of the youngest of the pirates swam out to the Jet Ski, which had a platform on the back to load up passengers. He sped it up onto the shore and three other boys helped him quickly turn it around to take Bobby out to the Zodiac. After nine other trips, the Zodiac was filled. Payments of one hundred bucks a head plus a surcharge for the kayak were given to Bobby.

## KISS THE SAND!

Tied to the back of the Zodiac, Corky held on for dear life. So did we in the boat with rough seas and a captain who threw caution to the wind, taking us airborne several times. What would have taken hours under good conditions in Corky only took a half-hour by Zodiac. Arriving in Hanalei, I didn't get out of the boat and kiss the sand, but I wanted to. I was thankful for being rescued and on land where we could load up our things and drive home for a good night's sleep.

Corky, Brian, and I survived this misadventure, albeit with a few more battle scars for Corky and a good story. Lesson learned: always have a Plan B and one hundred dollars cash a head for any adventure.

# MY NEMESIS

Whether meeting my former in-laws in Brazil or taking a solo walkabout through South America, many memorable travels were punctuated by run-ins with my nemesis. Although I've tried to be a Superwoman, my kryptonite is stinging insects. Whether it's a hornet in Minais Gerais, Brazil, or an *avispa* (wasp) in the Andes outside of Mendoza, Argentina, I'm allergic to it.

As a kid, my mother not only raised sheep but also honey bees. On countless occasions, I remember being stung and having red swollen welts, but I never needed an EpiPen, which is an injection of epinepenrine that can reverse severe allergic reactions to stings, peanuts, or other. However, over the years and with more insect stings, I've become a believer in the saying that however hard you try, you end up like your mother. And my mother always had tremendous reactions to bee stings. In fact, while she was pregnant with me, she was stopped in her car by a local police officer because of her lead foot. Yes, my mother is notorious for speeding. On her way into town for errands and seven-months pregnant, she was covered from head to toe in bee stings. Not only was she swollen from the summer heat and her pregnancy but also from a mass attack of bees from her hive. As she rolled down the window to hand over her license and registration, the officer took one look at her and stepped back. He glanced at the license and registration and said, "I'm going to let this one slide. Drive safely."

My mother never carried an EpiPen, but when she heard that my head swelled to the size of a basketball in Brazil, or that my arm broke out into blisters from a wasp sting, she said, "You better get an EpiPen." Did I listen to my mother? Oh, of course not. I had to learn the hard way.

## STUNG IN THE ETERNAL CITY

The sting that really tipped the scales happened in Rome on my second trip to the Eternal City as a tour manager. I was not only touring Italy but had to manage back-to-back trips.

First, I co-led a group of sixty people for ten days travelling from Rome to the Greek Isles and Turkey. Then after my co-leader returned to the States, I continued for a week in Rome and various Tuscan cities. Thoroughly exhausted from the first trip, I kept going, fueled by good Italian espresso until it was the appropriate time to drink great Italian wine.

On one particular day while still in Rome, the group had free time to tour museums, shop, visit the Vatican, or just rest. Although I would have preferred to snooze, I couldn't rest until the tour is over. So it was off on foot with a small group to a local food market for shopping and of course eating our purchases.

After a quick *pranzo* (lunch) at the market, I separated from the group to return to the hotel with one of the guests. As we passed the Coliseum, I felt a sudden prick on my left hand. Connected to the top of my hand was a small bee. I yelled, "God damn it. Ouch!" Although I tried to slap it dead, I didn't kill the bugger. Instead of having a leisurely walk back to our hotel on the famous Via Veneto, I made a beeline to the nearest *farmacia* where I got topical steroids to treat my blistering hand.

First item of business upon returning to the States: get an EpiPen.

| CUBA | CHPTR 51 |
|------|----------|

# SCALING COLISEUM WALLS

In passing the Coliseum, getting stung, and waiting at the pharmacy, my mind flashed back to my first visit to Rome. I was in college traveling with three other women. After spending most of our holiday break in Turkey and then taking a boat to southern Italy, we only had two days in Rome. That's like telling someone to read all of *Don Quixote* in one sitting!

It seemed the rest of the world was visiting Rome, too. The lines to go into places were unbelievably long, so we opted to walk and eat our way through Rome rather than wait in line. Yet how could we leave Rome without touring the Coliseum? It would be an embarrassment, right?

On our last night when the streets were relatively empty, it was time to find a good take-out place for pasta and a bottle of Chianti. I don't know which one of us had the idea, but we came up with a mischievous plan. *We'd break into the Coliseum.* At the time, the Coliseum had high iron gates, but these gates had two crossbars that make scaling them doable. The gates weren't secured with barbed wire or broken bottles; that would not be classy or look good in photos.

With assistance from our strongest accomplice from Indiana and the adrenaline of risking time in an Italian jail, all four of us jumped the gate. We all made it over with no injuries other than our hearts jumping out of our chests. We sneaked our way through the maze of dark hallways to get to the center of the Coliseum. Under the light of the moon, the stadium looked absolutely majestic. The shadows playfully painted a picture of what it would have been like in its day. I could imagine the whole stadium filled with water and boats engaging in battle, or gladiators fighting for their lives in front of cheering spectators *and* the emperor.

Afraid to draw the attention of guards walking around with flashlights, we moved in complete silence. However, after about fifteen minutes, our luck ran out when one of us (who will remain nameless but it wasn't me) took a photo using a flash. This alerted one of the guards to investigate.

We rushed to get back to our escape route, being as quiet as possible. This time, we were so scared, we all made it over the gate without the help of a boost. The pumping adrenaline was enough.

I don't recommend breaking into the Coliseum, but definitely don't leave Rome without seeing it. If you think we deserved punishment for what we did, well, we did. We didn't spend a night in a Roman prison, but *Roma* did get its revenge. Either on our way in or on the way out, one of us had stepped in dog poop. Yes, in climbing up and over the gate to our freedom, we got our hands smeared with *cacca*.

# TRAVEL LESSON: TRUST YOUR GUT MORE THAN THE GUIDE BOOKS

On that back-to-back tour of the Mediterranean when the bee stung me, I ended up in Turkey near the port city Izmir, which I'd visited nearly twenty years before. As I was organizing excursions to Ephesus as well as the Turkish *hamams* (baths), I looked with new eyes at the Turkish port, flag, and shops with their piles upon piles of Turkish rugs. Oh, how many good times and good stories I've had since that first trip. As I sat drinking an apple tea near the port, I laughed recalling my last taste of Turkey. What a doozy!

Traveling with the same mates who scaled the Coliseum walls, we started in Istanbul, stopped in Cappadocia, and departed from

Izmir for our continued trip through Italy. On this trip and for most of the two years I studied and lived in Europe, I used a well-known travel guide. It recommended a hostel in Izmir for our two-night stay on Christmas Eve and Christmas Day. Hostel Duvon seemed to be in a respectable area. Once we arrived, we split up into two rooms, left our bags, and hit the town.

## HOSTEL DUVON DIDN'T FEEL RIGHT

After a full day of sightseeing, tea drinking, and culinary experimentation including the Turkish version of *baklava* (a sweet desert) and *musakka* (like lasagna), we returned to our hostel to find a once-empty lobby filled with men sitting on couches smoking and drinking tea. As we continued to our rooms, we noticed some of the other "guests" seemed to be rather settled into their rooms. Strange. In particular, we caught a sneak peek of a room with a radio, ample décor, no suitcases, and full closets. It didn't look anything like our stark rooms with two twin beds, two large traveling backpacks, and clothes hanging to dry.

Leaving the hostel for dinner that evening, we walked through the smoke-filled lobby of men. As we sauntered down the street to find a bite to eat, we discussed the various red flags we'd noticed. In Turkey, or at least twenty years ago, it was uncommon for a group of young women to go out to dinner together, let alone ask for a drink of alcohol. But that night, we wanted to celebrate Christmas Eve. Stumbling on a restaurant that all four of us agreed upon for dinner, we felt safe there—temporarily. After we ordered, we pulled the waiter aside and asked him about this neighborhood and specifically about Hostel Duvon. He left the table to get the manager, Ahmet, who spoke a little English. He explained we were staying in a brothel.

Yes, you read it correctly—Christmas Eve in a Turkish brothel. Now, nothing says Christmas more than that!

## WHAT SHOULD WE DO?

Should we stay out all night in a city where it's uncommon to see women outdoors at that hour? Should we go back to the brothel and hope that strength in numbers works? Or what?

Before finishing our meals, Ahmet—a nice man, it seemed—invited us to stay in his apartment. We evaluated the plan: four young women, one complete stranger, Christmas Eve, and in a foreign country. No option seemed safe. We had to choose the lesser of all the bad plans. Plan B was to go with Ahmet.

Ahmet and his friend who owned a car took us back to the hostel, and we grabbed our bags and checked out. The owner was quite upset at us for cancelling, but who could blame us for not wanting to be in such a place? With all of our bags, we couldn't fit in one car so we hailed a cab. We four "savvy" travelers—escaping a hostel-turned-brothel with our bags packed like sardines in two cars—rode out to the suburbs of Izmir. We felt uncertain but hopeful that Plan B would be fine.

## WALNUTS AND SARDINES

Ahmet's apartment was in a rather unkempt cement high-rise that had an elevator but it didn't work. After walking up flights of stairs with our backpacks, we were "home" at his bare apartment. It had a Turkish bathroom (a hole in a porcelain slab with two foot grates), a small kitchen, and two rooms both spartanly furnished. One was his bedroom and the other a living room now turned into our bedroom for the night. As hospitable hosts, Ahmet and his friend began the "conversations" of the evening with an English/Turkish dictionary in hand. And in the spirit of the holidays, they brought us snacks. No, not chestnuts or eggnog, but walnuts in the shell and sardines recently caught and fried. The *sardalye* and walnuts were presented to us on a blanket of newspaper spread out in the center of the living room floor. We all sat down and gratefully dug in. Surprisingly, this was the first time I'd eaten a whole fish with bones and all. The sardines were absolutely delicious—a tremendous find, as I'm not a fish person.

We filled the night with stories told in a unique blend of English, Turkish, and sign language. The night came to an end as Ahmet graciously gave us blankets to keep warm in the cold apartment. However, something about the blankets was just foul. Yes, they stunk like a barnyard.

Regardless of the stinky blankets and being in a stranger's house, it felt better than being prey in the Hostel Duvon. By the way, we had become immune to the blanket smell by morning and, yes, we all smelled like a barnyard, too.

## THE SPIRIT OF CHRISTMAS

The next day, Christmas, dawned with new friends in a safe, not-so-strange apartment. In the spirit of Christmas, Ahmet and his friend helped us find another hotel—this time respectable and clean and not a brothel. We stayed in Izmir for two more days and saw Ahmet on one other occasion when he took us to a tearoom. We exchanged addresses and years later, I was still receiving "when you come back to Turkey" postcards.

So when planning your travels to Turkey or anywhere else, remember to trust your gut instinct about your surroundings and people you meet. And be wary of online and travel book resources. They can provide a good start, but their recommendations can backfire—as we found out in Turkey. Maybe I should have told alpha Karol about them when her online restaurant recommendation didn't pan out. It's hard to beat a story about a brothel on Christmas!

## CHPTR 53

# BIRTHDAY
# PRESENTS
# DOWN UNDER

It's common to have guests on tour celebrating a birthday, anniversary, retirement, divorce, graduation, or other milestones. In fact, I climbed Machu Picchu with a woman celebrating her seventy-fifth birthday. Countless couples have traveled to Cuba with me as an anniversary gift. Many singles have celebrated their divorces by cruising on a tour with me through the Mediterranean as well as Down Under.

## AT WORK ON MY BIRTHDAY

Although I don't make a habit of working on my birthday, one year it coincided with a multiple-week journey through New Zealand and Australia. It was my second time to lead tours on cruise ships in both of these marvelous countries. I was persuaded to work on my birthday because I already knew the tour, it came with a sizeable paycheck, and I had the rest of the holiday season off.

Starting in the warmer North Island of New Zealand and working our way down to colder, damper weather around the South Island, I felt my body take on a cold the farther south we went. (It seems every time I cruise, I get sick.) Regardless of using hand sanitizer and upping my dose of vitamin C, cruise ships are floating petri dishes. I would hedge my bets they pose a greater health hazard than teaching school or running a daycare center.

I arrived in Hobart, Tasmania, on my birthday with a severe chest cough, fever, and sore throat. My handy-dandy emergency Z-pack supply allowed me to skip visiting the doctor on board the ship. However, my first stop was a pharmacy to get lozenges. The selection of cough drops was quite surprising. They didn't come in flavors such as cherry, honey lemon, or menthol but only a unique butterscotch menthol. So when in Australia, do as the Aussies do, which includes butterscotch menthol cough drops. You might even try toast with Vegimite, a vegetable paste spread on toast like peanut butter but tasting like you licked a lawn mower. My verdict on both: YUCK!

## SPECIAL B-DAY EVENTS

The evening of my birthday, I received a card in my cabin with a reservation at one of the specialty dining restaurants. This gift from my entire group meant I'd be dining in style that night. It was a thoughtful gesture, even though I really wanted to settle in my cabin with hot chicken soup and a movie.

Changing time zones gave me a second chance to have a better birthday. For my friends and family (aka my clan) back in the States, my birthday was the following day. By our arrival time in Sydney on my second birthday, the antibiotics had taken root and I kicked the fever. Though I still was coughing, my sore throat had subsided thanks to the memorable Down Under cough drops. As we got into town, both my Facebook and iPhone had exploded with birthday messages from the States. Many asked, "What are you doing to celebrate your birthday?"

During my previous time in Sydney, I'd wanted to do the Sydney Bridge Climb. Some of my adventurous guests had done it, but due to timing and my responsibilities with other guests, I couldn't join them. However, this time, I would be leaving late from Sydney while all the other guests were departing in the morning. So that day, I would gift myself the Sydney Bridge Climb—an organized walk and climb to one hundred thirty-four meters above sea level for panoramic views of Sydney's harbor, Opera House, and skyline. Happy Birthday to me!

## PERSPECTIVE IS EVERYTHING

Finally—after a long, arduous trip with a challenging group of guests and a nasty chest cold—I said my farewells before everyone headed out to the airport. Then I was free to set out for the bridge tour.

On the warmest day of this entire trip, I zipped up a blue onesie jumpsuit, put on my microphone headset to listen to and communicate with the climb leader, and followed my climb mates to the start. With the traffic passing below us, it resembled the walk upon grates with a safety harness similar to my bungee jump off the Auckland Bridge a year earlier. Although this wasn't quite the same adrenaline fix as jumping off a bridge, it did get me in the zone. As I enjoyed the view, I realized I didn't have to look at my watch or meet with guests, restaurant managers, or bus drivers, I could be completely in the moment.

As I'd learned from my accident, perspective is everything. That's why, for me, adventure is my meditation. That birthday present and bridge climb itself provided the needed shift. I could forget about the trials and tribulations of the past weeks or missing my clan on my special day.

For your next milestone b-day, I suggest changing your view and gift yourself an adventure!

## CHPTR 54

# SURPRISE, CUBA, I'M BACK!

After a grueling autumn, a long three-week trip to Greece, Turkey, and Italy, then a short break followed by a repeat three-week trip to New Zealand and Australia over my birthday and Thanksgiving, I was ready for R&R. I was thoroughly exhausted and already on antibiotics for a nasty chest cold from cruise line travel. I needed a good dose of "me" time, perhaps becoming like a hermit crab for a while. This I found back in Kauai for the holidays and New Year.

This year, like previous years around the same time, I made a list of adventures and resolutions. Among them were to record audio versions of my first two books, write this *Cubicle to Cuba* book, and return to leading Cuba tours full-time. That would require me to use South Florida as my base, thus making it easier to help my dad.

The last goal had already been in the works with five trips to Cuba scheduled the following spring and summer. As far as the first goal, right after Christmas I headed into a studio not far from our *ohana* home and began recording the narration of my first book. Recording was fun, but there was another plus. I could be a hermit.

Yet, the process was more difficult than I'd originally thought. With a total of ten intense hours in the studio over multiple days, I had all the takes recorded. I knew it contained hundreds of mistakes, from mispronounced words to a sneeze or not enough contrast between my voice and another character's voice. So I hired an audio editor who would do the edits while I recorded my second book on my January trip to visit my dad in Florida. He just so happened to be a retired theatre and speech professor with expertise in the matter at hand.

While in Florida, I set out to record my second book, *With New Eyes*, from my father's home. With his help, we converted his walk-in closet into a soundproof room. It even had a red light outside to alert him that I was recording. I don't know what it is about me and small spaces, but I tend to crank out lots of work from them. That began at UW-Madison and continued on to writing multiple books from small makeshift home offices.

## CUBA CALLS AGAIN

One day on a break, I checked my email and received another call to Cuba to fill in for a colleague who had an emergency. My only other tour for later that spring was a March cruise to Europe with close to a hundred people. I immediately responded, "Yes, I'm available." That afternoon, I set the paperwork in motion arranging visas, tickets, and accommodations.

Donning my Cuban straw hat and pulling my well-packed behemoth, I showed up at our Miami hotel to meet my group of twenty travelers. All their visas and tickets were in order—except for one problem. No ticket or visa for me, although there was one for my colleague, Jason Clayton, whose place I was taking.

Since I knew the team at the charter airline, I immediately phoned them as well as my boss at the agency. By the time I brought the group to the airport, the airline had a visa and ticket in my name. But regardless of the previous paperwork submission and change at the Miami airport, my Cuba connections wouldn't know about my arrival. The hotels, guide, and driver were expecting Jason Clayton.

## ECHOES OF THE BOSTON MARATHON

This felt like a playback of running the Boston Marathon in 2004. The Boston Marathon is a race you must qualify for by running another official race in a time fast enough to qualify. Alternatively, you could run as part of a charity and raise thousands of dollars, know someone who works for a major sponsor, or run without an official number as a "bandit."

I had begun training in the fall of 2003 through the winter and ran in the Patriot's Day Race the next April. Although I could have dedicated more time to the already time-consuming race training by raising money, I decided to run as a "bandit." That was until one of my girlfriends in Boston, Nikki, told me her boyfriend, Mark, worked for John Hancock, the major sponsor. Because of an injury, Mark wouldn't be running and happily gave his number to me, I ran the Boston Marathon as Mark. Similarly, people at each hotel as well as at the Cuban travel agency would be expecting Jason Clayton. It all worked out.

Thank you, Mark, for your race number in 2004 and *gracias*, Jason, for allowing me to be your stunt double in Cuba.

## CHPTR 55

# OMG VERTIGO

Early in 2016 on a visit to Kauai, I had just lain down in bed and looked to the right when a wave of dizziness hit me. As if I were walking through the desert with waves of heat, my vision blurred. Because it passed in a few seconds, I dismissed it as a one-time thing—until it happened again. In the hallway the next day, I looked up and to the right at Brian to give him a kiss before work. An intense feeling plus clouding of my vision struck me. I held onto Brian thinking I might faint. Worried, he walked me to the bed where I was able to return to feeling normal. What was going on?

As this continued over the next week, I decided to see a doctor upon my return to Florida and before my first tour of the year. Was this a side effect of my accident seven years before? I figured as I aged, I would notice pain and perhaps even experience arthritis in my neck, shoulder, and upper back due to the accident. I never imagined other possible problems because I'd been living a very healthy lifestyle.

## DOCTOR'S EXAMINATION

Having changed health insurance companies the year before, I found a new primary care doctor in Florida. At my first appointment, an African American doctor, chubby around the middle with glasses, entered the examining room a half-hour late. As he fumbled through my file showing my vitals from the nurse, I sat atop the examining table silently rehearsing the short version of my symptoms and history. Finally, he asked, "So what brings you in today?"

I explained the recent dizzy spells as well as the blunt trauma to my head and neck years earlier. In my mind, I assumed that red flags were waving about this new patient, pre-existing condition, and malpractice in his mind. The doctor calmly tested the strength in my hands as well as the movement and focus of my eyes, similar to what doctors did during my recovery. Both tests seemed normal, but then the true test came. He gently asked me to recline and look right while keeping my eyes open. Just as I did that, the dizziness abruptly started. He repeated the same test twice on the right as well as on the left, confirming a diagnosis of vertigo. As he returned to his desk, he talked and typed out the next steps.

"I'm going to give you this prescription for the dizziness. However, I also suggest you see a neurologist as well as get your eyes checked."

"Are there side effects to the prescription for dizziness?" I asked.

"It may make you sleepy. You can continue to do as you have been, just stopping and letting the dizziness pass. However, because of your history, I'll refer you to a neurologist as well as an ophthalmologist to rule out other issues."

"I have a neurologist I trust, Dr. R in Plantation. He knows my history. Could you write the referral to him?"

"Sure. I'm very familiar with Dr. R."

Although I left the doctor's office with a diagnosis, I didn't know the cause. How could I continue to live and work with vertigo? I was scheduled to be in Cuba in a week and on a cruise ship with nearly a hundred guests in little more than a month. How can I do any job with vertigo, let alone *my* job? OMG. Vertigo.

## RETURNING TO THE CAPTAIN

A familiar voice answered the phone at Dr. R's office. Tiff, a young African American receptionist and office manager, remembered me. At that time, I'd been a frequent flyer at his office but also a success case. When I met Dr. R in 2010, I had been rejected by dozens of doctors. So when Dr. R told me he would help me, he said, "I'm the captain of your ship." I cried in relief. Dr. R reassured me I didn't need to be the patient, healthcare advocate, *and* in charge of the complicated recovery. He took on that role.

Since being released from his care, I had seen Dr. R several times. When my first book was released, I stopped by the office to give him a signed copy, highlighting his quotation in the front. It reads: "Your accident wasn't a life change. The life change will be the path that you choose because of your gained perspective. You will know what you want from life, perhaps leaving the pre-accident life behind totally." Also, when my father left the rehabilitation center after his stroke, both he and I wanted a second opinion about regaining mobility in his right arm. Who did we trust? Of course, it was the captain, Dr. R.

When I walked into his office this time, I noticed a television playing a cartoon DVD and the reception desk had moved from behind a frosted glass window. Tiff greeted me and said, "Heidi, take a seat. Dr. R will be with you shortly." I noticed no one had an obvious condition like I did when I arrived in the spring of 2010. Wearing my back, chest, and neck brace, I'd looked like a storm trooper from *Star Wars*. Were they sizing me up, too?

Shortly after, an African American mother and her young son, probably six years old, were escorted to a patient room, leaving me to my own thoughts. Was this vertigo a side effect of my accident? Would there be a cure? Could this be a precursor to something worse?

After fifteen minutes, a young man in a white doctor's coat came out to get me. We entered a small corner examining room where Dr. R was facing a computer. He turned around, we hugged, and then he instructed me to get up on the table. He began by introducing the young man as a medical student and recapping my history as one of his best patients. Then he asked the inevitable question, "What brings you in today?"

I said, "I'm getting dizzy spells. I've seen my new primary care doctor who says it's vertigo, but he wanted you to examine me to see if it's something to do with my accident."

Like the other doctor, Dr. R did the same reclining maneuver, which I'd learned was the Dix-Hallpike test. This time, I experienced vertigo on both sides. Without fail, my head spun and vision blurred. Between each set, he gave me time to recuperate while he explained the symptoms that indicated BPPV (Benign Paroxysmal Positional Vertigo).

As he finished the test, I interjected, "After my recovery, I thought I would be fine until I reached a much older age. Is this happening because of my surgery and trauma to my head and neck?"

Pausing first as he typed notes into the computer, he then said, "This is not because of your accident and it's common when you get older. It's caused by crystals or otoconia in your inner ear that have moved."

Relief! At least this wasn't a precursor of something worse. I felt relieved. However, I was still getting debilitating dizzy spells. How could I be in charge of a tour with nearly one hundred people? I asked, "How can I get rid of the symptoms?" That worried me most.

"Look up vestibular exercises on YouTube. These exercises will force you to become dizzy. Over time, your body will compensate, thus decreasing your vertigo. However, remember to do them multiple times a day, and then come back here in three weeks."

As we hugged goodbye, he said, "I have a feeling, with your active lifestyle and the exercises, you'll be back to normal in no time."

"Thank you, Dr. R."

This visit to my captain reminded me how spectacular our

bodies are *and* how fragile life is. I rushed home to watch YouTube videos and get myself dizzy. By the time of my first Cuba trip and the cruise, I had dizzied myself out. The exercises worked. Dr. R did it again!

# LIVING IN THE MOMENT: WHY I LOVE CUBA

With all politics, economics, and anti-Castro talk aside, I believe Cuba and its culture offer life lessons for all of us. I have witnessed the perseverance of the Cuban people through shortages of water, housing, and transportation as well as limited quantities of toothpaste, diapers, and soap. Through thick and thin, my takeaway from Cuba is *appreciating the moment.*

Although I can explain this to you until I'm blue in the face, a more Cuban way to do so is through music. You may not be familiar with *"La Vida es un Carnaval"* ("Life is a Carnival") by the late and vivacious Cuban singer Celia Cruz, but I suggest reading the translated excerpt below and then listen to the music online. Try to keep your feet still (you can't):

Anyone thinking that life is unfair,
Needs to know that's not the case,
That life is beautiful, you must live it . . .
. . . Anyone thinking that life is cruel,
Needs to know that's not the case,
That there are just bad times, and it will pass.
Anyone thinking that things will never change,
Needs to know that's not the case,
Smile to the hard times, and they will pass.
Ay, there's no need to cry, because life is a carnival,
It's more beautiful to live singing.
Oh, Ay, there's no need to cry,
For life is a carnival
And your pains go away by singing . . .

As the song states, there are bad times, and they will pass. Yes, life obstacles come and will continue to present themselves; however, there is and always will be the moment. This understanding of "being in the moment" can be seen any night of the week with plentiful life outside of the home. I've seen every ocean boulevard or plaza lined with crowds of Cubans from each generation. They're enjoying good company, music, and dominoes without a cellphone in sight. I see this recipe for happiness repeat itself nightly.

## CULTURAL ELEMENTS OF CONNECTION

Although I don't have family roots in Cuba, I feel a deep connection to the two Cuban cultural elements of happiness and perseverance. From my *When All Balls Drop* moment, rock bottom, and losing it all in 2009, I persevered. And I not only survived but thrived. I chose to vie for the upside and be the architect of Life 2.0, which totally values happiness and living the moment.

I share this takeaway from Cuba as well as my own Post-Traumatic Growth story to inspire you. As you face life's obstacles, I encourage you to persevere and create happiness through whatever perspective you choose. As the song says, "Smile to the hard times, and they will pass." Yes, Cuba is a cultural example of living the mantra #LookUp every day.

# CUBANIZE IT!

In Cuba, jury-rigging is not only a necessity but also an art form. Menard's, Home Depot, and Napa Auto don't have locations in Havana or any of the other provinces. To be stereotypical, Cubans are inventors, jury-rigging everything from those 1950s car engines with Russian or Chinese parts, to making toilets flush a myriad of ways and washing machines last decades. If necessity is the mother of invention, Cubanizing is part of the Cuban DNA.

Regardless of the time of year, the city, or the fame of our hotels, our rooms needed Cubanizing, too. That's why customarily on the first breakfast at any one of our hotels, I'd sit at a table, grab a *café cubano*, make a mental note of all guests present, and call those I hadn't seen. I'd quickly scarf down a small *tortilla* (omelet) with fresh *fruta bomba* (papaya), guava, and mango. Afterwards, I'd do a throwback from *Home Improvement* (TV sitcom of the

1990s), putting on my "Heidi of Tool Time" hat and virtual tool belt, and I'd visit each table to learn the issues with each of the rooms. Some guests (aka angels and seasoned travelers) would be flexible, saying, "We can't expect to come to a developing country and get First World luxuries. We're okay with our room." However, the majority expected more, in spite of my discussion on our first evening explaining the differences between four-star ratings in Cuba and four-star ratings in the States, Europe, or South America.

By the end of breakfast, I had a list for the hotel's maintenance men and maids to Cubanize everything, from ACs, TV remotes, plumbing, shower heads, lights, windows, and doors. If the problem still existed upon our return to the hotel in the late afternoon, we played our musical rooms game. I prefaced it with this disclaimer: "All of the rooms are different. Some are fab, others drab." Then I crossed my fingers hoping that the second time, their rooms would have fewer issues or imperfections that my guests could overlook. Yes, at times, I switch my room with guests. I have even slept in three different rooms on a three-night stay on more than one occasion. As I said, I don't unpack.

## ALWAYS INVENTING

The term "Cubanizing" didn't only refer to maintenance or repair issues. It touched every facet of our trip, even the recipes. On various occasions, restaurants couldn't get butter for the breadbaskets to serve with each meal. Knowing that Cuban bread is dry and Cuban crackers no more moist than a piece of cardboard, the cooks would Cubanize a condiment depending on what was available. In mango season starting in late May, for example, they'd prepare mango chutney. On other occasions, they'd replace butter with a homemade garlic mayo, a tomato tapenade, or a *mojo* (garlic, lemon juice, oil typical marinade for meats). It reminded me that all-night grocery stores and megastores such as Costco and Super Wal-Mart were the reality in the U.S. but not in most countries around the world, especially Cuba.

Once large global megastores come in, the Cuba I know won't be the same, but there's certainly a need for them. When the U.S. embargo on Cuba is lifted, I imagine these big warehouse-sized stores will come, but buildings will need to be erected and roads or parking lots lain before they open. I see an easy Cubanized fix by bringing in a Home Depot barge. This would be like the tourism industry seeing cruises as a quick fix to having enough accommodations, food, and water for hundreds or thousands of additional people coming to any one of Cuba's port cities.

Does Cubanizing last forever? No, but it gets us by as we focus on the now and living in the moment.

# MY CUBAN
# CELL PHONE

Throughout my umpteen tours in Cuba, I had been asked by my Cuban friends to purchase unlocked phones for them in the States and bring them to Cuba. On one occasion, I said I would in exchange for a favor: I wanted a Cuban cell phone.

Although the American telecommunications companies announced they'd be opening in Cuba, it wouldn't be the best way to communicate using an American number and incurring roaming charges. So Maylene, my Cuban friend and confidant in Cienfuegos, sent her brother, Alejandro, to ETESCA to open a mobile number for me with a small, unlocked phone nicknamed *chiquito* (mini).

Well into the twenty-first century, who thought I'd be reverting to keyboard texting like I did in the late '90s? This iPhone addict found using a *chiquito* a challenge. Imagine—it took nine clicks to send the message "Hola."

Regardless, *chiquito* gave me the freedom to call the States from whenever and wherever for emergencies as well as give advance notice to our guide or hotels if we were delayed, lost, or faced a million other hiccups. I still dealt with hurdles having a Cuban cell phone. It wasn't a plan with unlimited minutes and texts and, like the Internet cards, it tracked usage by the minute. That meant I'd need to go to an ETESCA shop or kiosk to purchase a card when my minutes were getting low.

However, like most things in Cuba, I found a workaround, which I took advantage of when I returned to the States. Multiple foreign companies would allow customers to purchase phone time online at a discounted rate. So when I learned about this *"recarga"* online and the sales they ran around Mother's Day or holidays, I'd get random email messages from Cuba to recharge my friends' phones online as well as mine.

I've confessed my iPhone addiction. Whenever my phone doesn't work, I go crazy. Other than my health or the health of my clan, my phone is a necessity. In Cuba with no working iPhone, I made this little Cuban phone my lifeline.

For example, on one of my trips, all of a sudden I didn't have the ability to send texts. I could receive calls and make calls, but I couldn't send texts—a problem. Everything in Cuba we do on the "el cheapo," which means it's cheaper to communicate with everyone via text than phone. I asked my friends, their teenage daughters, and even the driver to take a look at my phone settings, but to no avail. I'd have to find time to stop by an ETESCA store days later in Havana to rectify this problem.

In Old Havana only blocks from Hemingway's Ambos Mundos Hotel, I found the Obispo ETESCA office. Once the security guard allowed me to enter the building, I awaited my turn for one of the technical specialists to assist me. A beautiful young woman at the first desk waved me over. She took my phone, went into settings, and gave it back to me in less than thirty seconds. She told me it was a "*malconfiguración.*" I knew I hadn't changed the settings—unless by mistake through butt-dialing.

I thanked her with a smile and a cone of *mani* (peanuts). I needed to be more careful. No more butt- or pocket-dialing.

## CHPTR 59

# THREE BOTTLES
# OF RUM ON
# THE WALL

The job of tour manager starts anywhere, from a few days to a couple weeks, before the tour date. For tours I repeat, I got the pre-trip down to a science—only one afternoon of errands. I'd buy and pack the essentials: ponchos for the entire group, bug spray, hand sanitizer, and a bucket of earplugs. For new tours, I'd do the same shopping, but also spend the weeks leading up to the trip researching, making reservations for group dinners, and printing maps and necessary information. (I didn't know when or if Internet connections would be available.) Whether it's an eight-day or twenty-day tour, unpaid pre-work is needed, thus lowering my average hourly wage to less than minimum wage. Add to that the post-work, which is mostly unpaid paperwork. It ranges from the dreaded expense report to customer service logs, or for Cuba, a multiple-page account documenting the people-to-people educational activities on the tour to be submitted to the U.S. Treasury Department.

The majority of the time, the job of tour manager in my high-alert triage mode ends when all of the guests have arrived safe and sound in our final airport with baggage and connecting flights arrangements complete.

## NOT QUITE SAFE AND SOUND

That's not what happened on a particular trip to Cuba with a group of healthcare professionals from the New York area. At the Havana airport, I started to let my guard down. The group had checked in and passed through security and passport control. Check! We boarded the plane and left on time. Check! Everyone was coming back healthy. Check!

But things fell apart when we arrived at the gate in Miami—or, better said, they just fell. You know that announcement from the flight attendant that states, "Be careful in opening the overhead bins as some objects may have shifted in flight." In a rush, one of my guests grabbed his bag from an overhead bin behind him, but he suddenly lost his grip. His bag carrying three bottles of Cuban rum from the duty-free shop fell directly on the head of another of my male guests—a young man about twenty-five years old. Ouch!

Seated three rows behind the afflicted guest, I stood up and rang various call lights. A female flight attendant responded as I looked back shouting, "Three bottles of rum landed on my guest's head. We need ice for the swelling." Promptly she returned with ice. While everyone deplaned, including the guest who dropped the rum, I remained with the injured man. So did his father, an orthopedic surgeon.

Although I'm no doctor, I know the warning signs of blunt hits to the head: dizziness, loss of sight, and excessive swelling. As his father did a quick assessment of his son, I asked the attendant for wheelchair assistance. The wheelchair arrived and whisked us all through customs swiftly. Fortunately, an hour later, the young man only had swelling and a bit of pain. Neither his father nor I could continue to his gate with him for his connecting flight, but we both stressed that if he had any dizziness to immediately get the airport paramedics.

In saying our farewells, he said with a tease, "At least it wasn't a thousand-pound tree limb." I laughed and smiled, saying, "Who knew that Cuban rum bottles could be deadly weapons! *Hasta luego.*" (See you later.)

# CHPTR 60

# LESSON IN CUBAN PUBLIC RELATIONS

The role of a public relations (PR) person is to strategically manage the image and thus the communications of a person, group, or organization. Before leaving Cubicle Land, I did various PR gigs in the travel, technology, and start-up areas. I was responsible for creating a favorable image of the companies, building win-win alliances, and presenting the upside of any hiccup. You may have heard the term "spin doctor"—a person who presents the favorable side to an audience that might be investors, partners, or media representatives. I was that person. I wouldn't say I was manipulative, but I had to craftily mask mistakes with enough white noise—good deeds, success stories, and more—to send a positive message.

Since hanging up my full-time PR and marketing hat, I have

taken on other roles. Still, my watchful eye has been set for captivating PR examples. Regarding the relations between Cuba and the U.S., I witnessed loads of interesting PR. It ranged from reports about the Bay of Pigs with Cubans touting the defeat of the Imperialist Yankees to the use of the word "blockade" or *bloqueo* instead of embargo. It all speaks wonders.

## SPIN DOCTORS

Fidel Castro is a skilled lawyer, writer, and orator, all skills that support a strong PR effort. With the change of a word, he and his spin doctors can shift the perception of an almost sixty-year *embargo* of goods toward Cuba into an intentional *blockade* of any goods coming into Cuba. Castro's team of cheerleaders and PR professionals has certainly sugarcoated the Cuban side, blacklisting the big bad world power to the north.

Meanwhile, the mainstream U.S. press doesn't cover Cuba unless a hurricane passes over it or Castro is ill. It's as if Cuba— only ninety miles from Key West—didn't exist! That was until Beyoncé and Jay-Z traveled to Cuba in 2013. Their PR effort made it Cuba-licious. Since, Cuba has been hot, hot, hot: Obama meeting with Raul in Havana, Tampa Bay Rays playing *pelota* (baseball) in Cuba, and even a Rolling Stones concert.

## CUBA | CHPTR 61

# HOT, HOT, HOT

No one should be surprised to hear that temps in Cuba are hot. Granted, it's not Death Valley, but it's the Caribbean where the combined humidity and heat can be stifling, without much respite. Even stoic travelers from Arizona who are used to dry heat, and those from Florida who are used to humidity, have complained about Cuban weather. Air conditioning everywhere has spoiled the modern world. In Cuba, though, air conditioning is a luxury. Most of the restaurants and stores don't have it, but hotels and tourist buses usually offer AC to provide a break.

However, there is no break for the average Cuban home. Window air conditioners, purchased with CUCs, are expensive. Thus, Cubans prioritize purchasing appliances in this order: fridge, washing machine, TV—the Holy Trinity of appliances. Only very fortunate Cuban families have an AC window unit.

## CUBA 101

As part of my welcome briefing that I call Cuba 101, I talk about how having a hat and an *abanico* (fan) is essential without AC. Some guests cleverly bought portable fans to wear around the necks. However, most people think they're already used to the heat until they hit the Cuban airport—no air conditioning and almost one hundred percent humidity. This was the case on all of my spring and especially summer trips to Cuba. The email below sent to my clan expresses my reaction to Cuba in the summer.

*Subject: hot hot hot*

*Message: All I can say is that it is hot hot hot. Think Florida without air conditioning. My hair is curly. I'm using my fan like a debutant. The passengers are melting, too.*

*Besos, (Kisses)*

*Heidi*

Just like Yislaine taught me, I had a Cuban solution to the heat: one mojito followed by a cold shower.

Speaking of cold showers, here's another belief I have about travel: Travel is like sex.

# TRAVEL IS LIKE SEX

*"Travel is like sex. There are thousands of ways to do it. It just depends on how you like it." – Unknown*

Whether traveling in a large group or smaller intimate family/ friend scenarios, each traveler, me included, likes different places, activities, food, and drinks that hit a chord with us personally. If you've ever traveled with others, you know this is true. Some prefer leisurely mornings, others pound down a local coffee and hit the ground running, and others burn the midnight oil at the clubs. If you can find a special clique or travel companion who embraces your style, you're lucky. And you're probably in the minority.

We all have horror stories of travel companions gone awry! But bad experiences make good stories, for sure.

## PLAYFUL TRAVEL EXAMPLES

Let me give you playful examples of travel being like sex.

Perhaps someone just wants a *one-day stand* in a location, hitting the major sites and moving on. Wham bam thank you Amsterdam! Others prefer to experience the cuisine, music, and dance of the destination ahead of the trip as a warm-up or *foreplay.* While one-day-stand travelers are showered ready to take on another city and those in foreplay are just warming up, there is another camp of traveler. These travelers prefer to experience the culture at a long, leisurely pace as they *take it slowly.* They enjoy the destination more and more as they learn about the area, people, cuisine, and customs. The slow travelers don't rush; they want the experience to last forever—a Tantra version of travel.

## THEN THERE'S SOUVENIR ENVY

Also, don't be fooled. You can experience *souvenir envy.* Travelers can be envious of others' purchases of jewelry, clothing, or works of art. (Think of locker-room scenes and secretly comparing sizes of phalluses.)

Like a man on Viagra, I could go on and on and on with this analogy. But no good travelogue ignores the topic of sex.

**CHPTR 63**

# THE PR WAY TO SAY "HURRY UP"

Just like any government, brand, or celebrity can mastermind a great PR plan, I use wordsmithing finesse to my advantage when I lead a tour. In any group travel regardless of the destination, age group, gender, or motive, the group IQ goes down. As stated earlier, everyone is on "brain-cation." However, another thing is certain. If you're a tour manager, you won't get through the aggressive itinerary that agencies put together if you're not a clock Nazi.

While wearing my timekeeper hat, on Day One I ask everyone in the group to synchronize their watches to mine or at least make sure our phones have the same time. That way, on Day Two, Three, or Four someone doesn't go shopping for an additional half-hour while a bus filled with passengers twiddling their thumbs waits. Being a clock Nazi is constantly required at every stop along the way. So I've found a way to politely say "Hurry up" other than "Get your ass moving." (Although it would be fun to say, my evaluations and tips would reflect it as a poor choice.) I say, "Giddy up."

## "GIDDY UP!"

This favorite PR saying comes from the TV sitcom *Seinfeld* and the character Kramer who says, "Giddy up!" Who doesn't smile after hearing that? For emphasis, I even add a quirky head motion and kick. If I need to do a second call, especially in Cuba, *"Vámonos"* works wonders. I've also been known at meal times to give a proactive five-minute warning like this: "It's potty time. No, not party time, but time to hit the restrooms. The train is leaving the station in five."

## TURN INTO A SHEPHERD

Once it's time to board the bus, I remove my clock-Nazi hat and become a shepherd or herder. This hat comes quite naturally as I was named Heidi after the book that takes place in the Alps. Since my childhood home was a hobby farm with sheep, my parents decided it would be cute to have a little girl named Heidi playing among their flock.

Now, depending on the age and agility of the group members, loading the bus takes anywhere from fifteen minutes to a half-hour. God only knows why it takes so long, but in an emergency, I know they'd do it faster than what I've witnessed.

Just like herding a flock, I circle round gathering the shutterbugs who needed one last shot, and those Internet addicts who needed one last send from a free Wi-Fi hotspot. The whole process can cause one delay after another, which is when I say a polite, "Let's rock and roll."

Regardless of what comes out of my mouth, though, in my head I say, "Come on. Hurry the f*#@ up!" I count and recheck with the *compay* system, and then say to the driver, "*Vámonos. Apurate.*" (Let's go. Hurry up!)

# MY TOTEM POLE AND DIVERSITY DOLL

Although my favorite souvenirs from all of my travels are recipes, I *am* a girl at heart. On occasion, I spot a small piece of jewelry I can't live or leave without. In particular, I'm interested in silver charms for my charm bracelet that once belonged to my mother and was gifted to me. With all its charms, both hers and mine, this bracelet has become heavy, so I expanded from a charm bracelet to a charm necklace. (Bonus: It doesn't get caught on my clothes like my bracelet does.)

I now have charms from around the globe: a surfboard from Kauai, a silver fern from New Zealand, a boomerang from Australia, a fleur-de-lis from Florence, an evil eye from Greece, and a silver coin from Cuba. Both the bracelet and necklace display charms that mark milestones in my life as well as favorite places and activities. In a way, it is my totem pole telling my story through pictures of places and events that have shaped my life.

## A FAVORITE GIFT FOR TINY VIPS

However, at times I've needed something other than a recipe or silver charm, especially for my goddaughter, Ali. My favorite gift from Cuba for her was handmade and came with a lesson. At local handicraft markets, women showcase their topsy-turvy cloth dolls—on one side a black woman and the other side a white woman. One side of the doll wears a bold dress and hair in braids while the other has a wrap like women wore in the slavery and sugar mill days.

What a great diversity lesson! This doll highlights that we are all one, regardless of color, size, or shape.

I gifted one of these dolls to Ali, who is *mulata* herself from Haitian and French-Cuban parents. And as other tiny VIPs have entered my life, I've made it a habit to bring back a doll for each of them. Not wanting their parents to feel left out, I bring adult gifts as well—Cuban rum and cigars.

# WEAKEST LINK OF THE TOUR

The tour management business relies heavily on the local tour operator or agency that provides local guides, transportation, and drivers. More times than not, I get off the plane not having worked with a particular guide or driver before. I cross my fingers and toes that 1) they are where they are supposed to be, and 2) we work well together.

For the most part, those who become local guides are "people" people—extroverted, easy to get along with, and all-around good eggs. They have studied history and languages. Some have hard-to-understand accents while others speak like the girl or boy next door. Local drivers are a bit more of a mixed bag. Some are pleasant, but many have chosen to drive a bus full of foreigners so they don't have to speak—not even to me. Unless I was traveling in a Spanish-speaking country, getting to know local drivers in

Greece, Morocco, and Turkey happened through translation by my local guide. Unfortunately, I didn't get to know them well; that opportunity was lost in translation. All personalities aside, when on tour, the people I rely on most can either be dreams to work with or epic failures.

For example, Yislaine was a doll. She and I became family. My tours in Cuba with her were not without hiccups, but we became the "A team." On the other hand, while on tour in Rome, our group of thirty guests was matched up with a local Italian guide, Guido, for a panoramic bus ride followed by a walking tour of the Trevi Fountain, the Pantheon, and Piazza Navona. He falls into the "epic failure" category.

## LEFT BEHIND

Guido was in his early fifties, spoke English well, and arrived relatively on time—for an Italian. After our spin around the city but before getting off the bus, Guido and I agreed upon a general outline of the walking tour starting at the Trevi Fountain and progressing to the Pantheon. I had been through the area the previous day but stressed that we needed to stay together—he leading the group and I pulling up the rear.

Once off the bus, our group proceeded to the world-famous Trevi Fountain. Although it was under construction and covered with scaffolding, flocks upon flocks of tourists just like us needed to throw a coin into the fountain, of course, to guarantee a return trip to Rome. It should take only a moment to toss a coin over your shoulder, but with thirty people doing it *and* capturing the moment on camera, it seemed like it took eons.

That's when Guido became impatient. He wanted the group to

move on. After counting all of our guests at least three times among the hordes of other tourists, we were off, again he leading and I pulling up the rear.

Although Guido spoke English and knew his history, overall he failed at his job that day. Why? He broke the number one rule: *don't lose a guest.* And he didn't lose only one guest but sixteen of us, including me! Rushing across streets and making turns we hadn't discussed beforehand, Guido simply left the rest of us behind.

## GOING INTO TRIAGE MODE

That's when I went into triage mode. As I led the group to the next stop, the Pantheon, I got out my cell to call Guido. But wait. I had the driver's number and the office number but not Guido's. How could I have forgotten it? *Remain calm.* I called the tour operator's office while my fifteen guests went inside the Pantheon, used the restrooms at a local cafe, or made another gelato stop.

Luckily, I spoke directly with the owner, Shannon, a Canadian woman who had moved to Italy and joined forces with her long-time Italian boyfriend, Alexis. Shannon apologized and quickly hung up to call Guido. Almost instantly, she texted me a message that he was on his way—along with his cell number.

Roughly a half-hour after my call, we were all together again. Guido apologized. I was upset, and pulled him aside to say, "How can I trust you to lead my guests when you lost *me*? Let's continue on so we don't lose more time, and remember not to lose any of us."

## GOODBYE TO GUIDO

That afternoon, I was grateful to say *arrivederci* to Guido, the weakest link. The following day, we had a different driver and guide going to Tuscany. I got those cell phone numbers immediately. And I made it a habit from then on to get the numbers even before getting on the bus so I'd never forget again. On my next trip to Italy, I had to use them because 1) the guide (not Guido) lost part of the group again, and 2) we had two vans break down in five days, one in Rome, the other in San Gimignano.

Was there a hidden camera somewhere? How can the same company give me two guides who lose guests two tours in a row? How in the world did two vans break down in five days? What *sfortuna* (bad luck)!

# A SENSE OF COMMUNITY

A common question I hear from guests on my Cuban tours is "How have Cubans survived?" I could have given a long answer, but in essence, Cuban society has persevered, through the dark Special Period of the '90s and more than half a century of the economic hardships, because of community.

From sharing housing with multiple generations to having a CUC income of one family member working in tourism floating the family, Cubans look out for one another. What was once commonplace in the U.S.—such as borrowing a cup of sugar from a neighbor—is a way of life in Cuba. For example, someone has access to Internet at work and sends emails to other friends' families via that account. Or when the *bodega* doesn't have a certain product, they find a *guajiro* (country man) who has coffee, vegetables, fruit, pork, and eggs on his farm.

In the absence of having everything and living with what's available, the bonds among families, neighborhoods, and colleagues have become strong, even crucial to surviving. The richness of the sense of community is one of the benefits of the last almost sixty years but also whenever the going gets tough. When I went through my personal Special Period, I had to reprioritize. My health was first, followed by my relationships with my clan. Without them, I would not have triumphed.

I'd hedge my bets to say Cubans would say the same.

## CHPTR 67

# TAKE ME OUT TO THE BALL GAME

In Cuba, the national sport is not soccer like the majority of Latin countries. The sport of choice is none other than baseball or *pelota*. Each province has its team, from the *Industriales* (Industrialists) of Havana to the *Elefantes* (Elephants) of Cienfuegos, and *Naranjas* (Oranges) of Villa Clara. Although these team names aren't well known outside of Cuba, many Cuban baseball players have become world-renowned. Cuba's National Team, comprised of the best players from the provincial National Series teams, has competed internationally and won Olympic Gold multiple times.

Although originally brought to Cuba by American sailors, baseball isn't only America's pastime; it's also Cuba's. *Pelota* is part of the Cuban identity and life.

## BASEBALL VS. SOAP OPERAS

Many Cubans may not own all of the appliances a typical American household has such as a dishwasher, dryer, or air conditioner. But they always have a TV, their third priority after a fridge and washing machine. The battle in most homes occurs between the men and the women over *telenovelas* vs. *pelota*. Baseball season is almost year-round. The Cuban baseball season starts at the end of November and continues into May, while the Major League Baseball games replay on TV Sundays from April through October.

Although I have sung "Sweet Caroline" during the 7th-inning stretch at Fenway Park in Boston, I haven't attended a Cuban baseball game. I have passed the *Estadio Latinoamericano* (Latin-American Stadium) in Havana countless times, which is close to one of my guests' favorite stops, La Corona Cigar Factory and Store.

## NEW FORM OF INTERNATIONAL RELATIONS

Coincidentally, on my visit in the summer of 2016, the stadium looked a lot different. It had received a new coat of paint for President Barack Obama's attendance at the game between the Cuban National Team and the Tampa Bay Rays. The running joke among Cubans was to invite Obama every month to generate more changes.

Cuba didn't stop at Barack's visit; it put out the red carpet treatment for Michelle Obama, too. Before her visit to the Hemingway Museum, Finca Vigía, it got upgrades including new pavement, fresh paint, and marketing signs.

With baseball being such a large part of both U.S. and Cuban society, it's not surprising that *pelota* can perhaps be the new form of international relations. Maybe the U.S. Congress should take a lesson from baseball and serve peanuts and Crackerjacks at its next general meeting. "Take me out to the ball game. Take me out with the crowd."

# CUBAN WINE—
# NOT A HOME RUN

Although I enjoy trying local libations when traveling, my go-to favorite adult beverage is a glass of *vino*, whether white or red depending on the weather, food, and mood. Knowing that my home state of Wisconsin had been producing incredible wines recently, I thought Cuba had wine potential, too. If it could be done in the land of beer and brats, perhaps serving roasted pork with wine was on the horizon.

In Cuba, wine is offered at most restaurants whether government owned or in the private *paladares*. Primarily, the wines come from Chile or Spain—both places I know well, along with their wines including Rioja, Malbec, and Sauvignon Blanc. However, no wines in restaurants were local. When would I come across a domestic wine?

## A DRY RED DOMESTIC

On a morning visit to a local market where farmers sold fresh produce and meats, I noticed a vendor selling wine. Surprised, I looked at various bottles and labels describing the reds and whites as dry, sweet, or table wine. I asked the man about the five varieties and his favorite. He'd classified most of the others as sweet, to which I immediately turned up my nose. So I selected a dry red wine.

That evening after a full day of touring, I returned to my room with a borrowed wine key from the hotel's bar. The bottle didn't have a real cork but rather a plastic stopper about one inch into the bottle. I used the key to remove the stopper, thus opening my first bottle of domestic Cuban wine.

Then I turned on TV to CNN, dug into my stash of peanuts, and poured a glass of Cuban wine. I took a sip. Yuck! To cover up the taste, I ate several peanuts and took a big gulp of water. Is it really that bad or am I a wine snob?

I took another sip. Yep, it was flat, watered down, seemingly the worst wine I've tried. Granted, there was no vinegar taste, so it hadn't turned. It was simply bad *vino*! I shook my head and continued my R&R watching the boob tube with peanuts and water.

Cuban rum, pork, and coffee are outstanding, but the Cuban wines don't hit it out of the ballpark for me. *Vino cubano, no bueno!*

**CHPTR 69**

# CUBA IS COMPLICATED

The taboo topics of politics, religion, and you name it do get discussed when you spend anywhere from eight days to four weeks on end with guests. In the case of people-to-people educational tours to Cuba, a topic that's touched on is religion. And religion in Cuba is complicated.

Before the Revolution in '59, the majority of the population was Catholic stemming from Cuba's Spanish roots. Also, there were small pockets of other world religions and a hybrid religion called Santeria. This Afro-Cuban hybrid was formed when the slaves were forced to worship Catholicism. Instead of giving up their native religion, they hid their deities behind Catholic Saints.

Post-revolution, President Fidel Castro declared Cuba an atheist nation. In fact, the communist party would not allow religious people to join its ranks. At this time, many priests and nuns left the country because of it. Logically, religious practices declined. For nearly thirty years, religion was pushed under the rug or at least practiced in private.

However, when the Soviet Union collapsed and withdrew its economic support, Castro and his brother Raul softened their stance on religion. They knew that, to get through the Special Period, religion was a necessity.

## THE POPE'S 1998 VISIT

In a historic visit to Cuba in '98, Pope John Paul II helped resurrect the Cuban Catholic Church. Cubans came out of the woodwork for the Pope. Nearly a million Cubans attended mass in Havana's Revolution Square, sparking a renaissance of Catholicism.

Although there was a resurgence of Catholicism, a large percentage of Cubans didn't align themselves with one particular religion. As a result, some became atheists or even flip-flopped from Catholic to Santeria to atheist. One of my younger male guides, Daniel, who was born and raised in Old Havana, explained to me that even religion in Cuba is like baseball. "Most Cubans bat for Catholicism, but when the going gets tough, many change teams. When a family member is sick or other, they convert to or practice Santeria. Then, there are atheists. Those are the Cuban free agents."

The more I learned about Cuba from religion, politics, and history, the more multi-layered and confusing it got. I defer to Daniel, who answered many questions about Cuba by saying *"complicado."* I agree with him. Cuba is complicated.

# A MEMORABLE RUN

Part of my tour routine as well as personal travel includes taking a run through a town or city to get a different perspective of it—and to not end up with a roly-poly body after imbibing large amounts of pork, mojitos, and natilla.

I make a point of running in the early morning, the only part of the day I can count on carving out the time. For years, I've been doing this in Cuba, regardless of which town: Havana's Malecón, Miramar's Quinta Avenida, and the main drag, Prado, in Cienfuegos. Typically, I set my alarm for five-thirty, get dressed in my running attire, drink a glass of water, and brush my teeth. Depending on the time of year, I could be running in the dark or right at sunrise. I mentioned a memorable morning run in Havana with Reynaldo. Another memorable run happened in Cienfuegos on a Sunday morning in May 2016 at sunrise.

## A SUNDAY MORNING RUN TO REMEMBER

The streets were quiet, only an occasional car or moped with someone dressed in black and white riding to one of the hotels for work. I passed the marina, yacht club, and various *casa particulares* (private B&Bs), defined by an upside down anchor in blue for tourists and in rust-red hue for nationals.

As I got closer to the seawall, I noticed a park with benches next to a fast-food hangout. As usual, I'd run into groups of young men and sometimes an occasional young woman who had been out all night dancing and drinking. They assumed I was a tourist, not only from my looks but because Cubans didn't commonly run, especially early on a Sunday morning. The catcalls in English varied from "Hello!" to "Baby!" and lots of fake kisses. I went on, passing the mobile street cleaners—each man with his own garbage can on wheels and broom—as well as the bread deliveryman on his bicycle cart.

After about a mile and a half, I arrived at my turnaround point, the statue of the famous bandleader and musician from Cienfuegos, Beny Moré. I touched the tip of his baton for good luck—kinda like the Trevi Fountain for me but without coins.

## THE CITY CAME ALIVE

On the return trip, Cienfuegos started to come alive with people waiting for the bus, more cars moving, and many more people peddling. On this particular morning, I passed the seawall admiring the billboard with the lyrics from one of Beny Moré's hits, *"Cienfuegos es la ciudad que más me gusta a mí."* (Cienfuegos is the city that I like most.) I stopped momentarily to take my customary GPS shot, a photo of my feet on the seawall with the pink hue of the recent sunrise and the lining palm trees. (I started doing the GPS shot as a way to capture the moment, with me in the picture, before the selfie stick was invented. Yes, the photos indicate my exact location like a GPS, but with my feet serving as a frame of the image. Over the years, I've had to put myself it some pretty awkward positions to get these shots.)

## MORE THAN A CATCALL

As I resumed running, a group of four young men about eighteen years old was heading in my direction. They all were dressed in trendy jeans, sneakers, and nice shirts. One carried an almost-empty rum bottle. Another carried a mobile speaker. It was obvious they were drunk and had been out all night. I normally run right by a group like this without much more than a catcall. But this time, one of the young men scared me. He jumped into my path enough that I had to stop.

In that moment, his friend made the fake kissing sound to grab my attention and pulled out his "little man." Disgusted and scared, I bolted. I could hear their laughter as I ran away, but I didn't turn around until I was close to the security booth of the yacht club a quarter mile away.

## WHAT AM I SUPPOSED TO DO WITH THAT?

Later in the day, I retold my story to my friend Maylene and my driver Yoan. They laughed but were shocked it hadn't happened earlier. Maylene joked and asked what "it" looked like. I laughed looking up from my Cuban coffee and responded that I didn't take the time to look. Yoan, our token man, knew the only way to deal with an exhibitionist was to insult him. He suggested I say the next time, *"Esto para qué me sirve?"* (Literally, how can that serve me, but better said, "What am I supposed to do with that?")

My virgin experience with a flasher made the run memorable, but the "it" was not.

# RETURNING TO WHERE IT ALL STARTED

After nearly twenty trips to Cuba, I still hadn't returned to where everything started. I had passed La Ferminia umpteen times in our *guagua*, but never did our tour dine there. Just nearby, I wondered if Angi and Alexis still ran the *casa particular*.

On my last tour to Cuba before the summer in 2016 nearly four years since my visit, I called the mobile phone number written on Angi's and Alexis's business card. Angi answered, shocked to hear from me. Rightfully so, as I hadn't stayed with them for more than a few nights years ago. I asked if she would be around Tuesday afternoon, which was the only free evening I had on that particular tour. Both she and Alexis were retired, so she agreed to be at the house, repeating the address and directions to get to her home off the main thoroughfare through her Miramar neighborhood to Quinta Avenida (5th Street).

Tuesday afternoon, it was raining cats and dogs (*lloviendo a cántaros* = raining jugs). The streets were filled with puddles, some too deep to cross in cars. The rain gutters of the houses struggled to handle the deluge. I imagined *Habaneros* inside their homes closing windows and moving buckets and plants around the house to catch the drops of water coming through any leaks from Cubanizing the roof, windows, or doors.

I ran from my ride to the carport where Alexis's old blue car was parked. At the main door, only the screen door was closed. I shouted, *"Buenas tardes, Angi . . . Alexis."* From another room, out popped Angi, a petite, dark-complected woman in her sixties in bare feet wearing shorts and a T-shirt. She hadn't changed a bit.

Angi opened the door and said, *"O Heyde, te recuerdo."* (Oh Heidi, I remember you.)

I removed my wet sandals and hugged her. Like always, I brought a little gift, a bag of chocolate candies. I gave it to her explaining I wanted to swing by to say hi as well as thank both she and Alexis. She looked puzzled.

## MY SAME ROOM

I told her that because of my previous stay at her house, I started a new job leading tours to Cuba, and that I was writing a book. I shared, *"Empieza en La Ferminia para Nochevieja."* (It starts in the La Ferminia restaurant on New Year's Eve.) She smiled and led me to my room. It was still the same double bed, refrigerator, and bathroom. Angi noted they'd added on two rooms for rentals and asked me to follow her.

Then Alexis appeared after returning from an outing. Angi filled him in on the *yuma* (American). I told him I'd enjoyed the meal of roasted pork and mojo he had prepared for me years before. That jogged his memory. He replied, "*Estaba lloviendo esa noche también.*" (It was raining that night, too.)

They offered me *café cubano*. I knew it wasn't socially correct to decline, but my ride was waiting for me. I had to make another stop in the area. As I put on my shoes, they gave me a brand-new business card and asked me to bring them guests.

## RESOLUTION MADE AND KEPT

That evening, I returned to La Ferminia. Entering the restaurant, I saw photos on its walls of Fidel Castro, a famous Cuban ballerina named Alicia Alonso, and even Stephen Spielberg, the American director. I passed the bar to the patio where I'd sat that *Nochevieja* (New Year's Eve) under the same banyan tree. I ordered a mojito from the waitress. As I watched her prepare it with just enough sugar, Havana Club three-year-old rum, soda water, mint, and a splash of bitters, I explained who I was and why I was taking photos. Then I took a sip, relishing the taste and the moment.

Little did I know that, by making a resolution to escape Cubicle Land and to travel and write more, Cuba would be a big part of that transition.

## CHPTR 72

# BLOWN HOME

After taking the summer off from leading tours to Cuba, I jumped in with both feet on a hairy new adventure.

As I met my next Cuba tour group in Miami, a tropical storm was brewing in the Atlantic and heading toward the Caribbean. We started our nine-day trip in Havana as I watched Hurricane Matthew slowly dance and blow around the Southern Caribbean. The weather models were so varied and unpredictable, I could have thrown spaghetti at a map to outline Matthew's path better. One had it hitting Cuba, another scarring Haiti, and another going right between both islands heading for the Bahamas and eventually South Florida.

Was I scared? Of course, I was apprehensive about it hitting our location in Cuba. I used any spare moment in the hotel to watch the Weather Channel and log into my email to get updates from our tour headquarters.

## EFFECTS OF HURRICANE MATTHEW

Halfway through our trip, Hurricane Matthew reached Category Five with a predicted landfall on Eastern Cuba, hundreds of miles from our beach stay in Varadero and even farther from our Havana departure. However, I started to see the bigger picture. Matthew might not affect us in Cuba, but it's flirting with us. As the storm crawled from Cuba and smashed Western Haiti continuing onto the Bahamas, the course took a dramatic turn to the West—not for Havana but toward South Florida. OMG!

Worried about my father in his home outside of Fort Lauderdale, I asked a friend to board up his house. I had to roll with Matthew's punches. I didn't know if I would need to stay in Cuba or if I would arrive in Miami early enough to get to Fort Lauderdale to pass the storm with him. Things were getting complicated!

## AIRPORTS CLOSING

Day by day, it looked as if we were going to run right into Matthew's path. And, as my group and I waited at the Havana Airport for our departure, we would be flying right into the storm. Would it be better to get to Miami or stay in Cuba? The airport to the north of Miami, Fort Lauderdale, had already closed at ten-thirty that morning. The airport in Miami was already scheduled to close at two in the afternoon, and we were still in Havana at twelve thirty. Yikes! It was almost time for a mojito or three.

Before I lost all hope, I received a text from my Cuban connection in the airport office saying that our plane from Miami was about to land. She clarified it was heading back to Miami after a quick turnaround. In fact, our flight from Havana was the last one allowed to arrive at Miami International Airport. We landed at just after two o'clock, with a grateful round of applause for the pilots.

## THE EERINESS OF MIA

Upon deplaning, we had arrived at an airport terminal I didn't recognize. Like being in the Twilight Zone, there were no lines at customs. The officials were waiting only for our plane. Once we had our luggage, no taxis or shuttle buses could be found. Although it was a tad eerie, quite honestly, it was the most pleasant MIA experience I've ever had. MIA is typically a nightmare: long security and customs lines at any hour, any day of the year.

I hedged my bets that with nothing more than heavy winds and rain, I could get safely to Broward Country and my dad. As my guests' flights out of Miami had been cancelled, my agency had set up reservations for the entire group at an airport hotel. Once I arranged a special shuttle for them, I quickly evaluated my options. I didn't want to spend a night in Miami with my group knowing I was only twenty miles from Dad.

## CUBAN DRIVER RESCUED ME!

After a week without access to the Internet on my phone, I immediately called Uber and requested a ride. Within minutes, not only did one appear, but he called me asking if I spoke Spanish. Well, yes, *hablo español*. On a day when no one else would help me get home, a young Cuban man who came from a long line of taxi drivers took me home safely. We talked the entire time about his home on the outskirts of Havana.

When I arrived at my father's home, we both hunkered down for a long night that never came. We were lucky. Matthew once again danced around my whereabouts by moving farther northeast.

I owe immense thanks to my community of South Florida and Cuban friends. This story wouldn't have a happy ending without them, especially my Cuban knight in shining armor.

# EPILOGUE

At the time I was introduced to Cuba—on January 1st, the celebration of the triumph of the Revolution—I was thirty-three years old, almost the same age as Fidel in '59 when he began governing Cuba. However, I too was leading a revolution or, better said, a transformation into my Life 2.0. As I resolved to make a career out of travel and writing that evening in Miramar, little did I know Cuba would continue to be a part of my transformation. This island took the role of my manna.

I left Cubicle Land for Cuba, touring Havana, Cienfuegos, Bay of Pigs, Santa Clara, Trinidad, Varadero, and Las Terrazas nearly ten times a year. Before long, Cuba became more of a home for me than Fort Lauderdale or Kauai. Over my years on the island, I was welcomed with open arms to my friends' homes and introduced to their families. They told jokes, taught me recipes, solved my travel hiccups, and even threw me a birthday party.

In this book, you have witnessed my transition from the corporate world to a life on the road in Cuba and beyond. Yes, this isolated Caribbean island opened doors for me to travel around the world, write about adventure, and even promote my books.

In spite of moving halfway across the world to Kauai, Cuba's lessons followed me, especially with the roosters. And when life threw me a curveball, Cuba was waiting for me time and time again. Every time I returned to Cuba and was welcomed by my friends and families there, I witnessed its transformation as well. During my transition to Life 2.0, I came to realize I was helping this island become Cuba 2.0.

Until our paths meet in Cuba or on another adventure,

Here's to looking up!

# ACKNOWLEDGMENTS

THANKS/GRACIAS TO MY CLAN! I COULDN'T HAVE
DONE THIS WITHOUT YOU!

Mom and Dad

My Partner in Crime (PIC), Brian

My Cuban *Familia*: Yislaine and Maylene

Adriana, Elaine, Caris, Diana, Jacqui, Rene, Karol, Will

Bryan, Patsy, Chrissie, Vila, Kris, Rose, Aerial, Ali

Lila, Cari, Alex, Wendi and Eve

Josh, Shannon, Polly, Nikki, Emma, Pete, Pierce, Ted

Dr. R, Virginia, Sandy

Dr. M and Dr. Z

Barbara McNichol Editorial

Yvonne Parks of PearCreative.ca

Maria Perilli at PPC Professionals

Zach Levendorf of Levy Media Marketing

Flavia Santos of Designarie.com

Here's to more good times and good stories together!

# ABOUT THE AUTHOR

Heidi Siefkas is an author, speaker, and adventurer with a powerful story that inspires others to overcome obstacles and live an adventurous life. Although she hangs her hat in Florida, she is never home for long, seeking other adventures and finding unique ways to tap into the power of perspective. Her speaking style, like her writing, is down-to-earth with just the right dose of sassy humor and wisdom.

Heidi speaks about:

- Overcoming Obstacles and Architecting a Life 2.0
- Living an Adventurous Life: How Adventure Can Be Your Meditation
- Climb to the Top of Your Game by Tapping into the Power of Perspective
- The Keys to Architecting Your Best Life
- Set Your GPS on Happiness—Where Will Your GPS Take You?
- Post-Traumatic Growth and the Art of Finding the Upside

# WHAT PEOPLE SAY ABOUT HEIDI'S TALKS:

"Insightful and inspiring—Your audience will be completely engaged and follow along effortlessly on her journey through life's adventures. You will feel sad, encouraged, and happy, leaving with tools to help you through your challenges."

**Ellen Latham MS**
Founder of Orange Theory Fitness Franchise

"A dynamic speaker with a unique ability to take a traumatic life event and create a positive light. Her interactive approach allows her audience to connect with her message."

**Yvonne Hasse**
Vice President of Suits, Stilettos and Lipstick

To schedule a presentation, event, or adventure with Heidi, please visit www.heidisiefkas.com. Use the contact page to send requests and details of the event, including when, where, why, and what you seek to achieve for your audience.

# WHAT PEOPLE SAY ABOUT HEIDI'S BOOKS:

*When All Balls Drop:*
*The Upside to Losing Everything*

*"A powerful chronicle of ultimate change and recovery."* – D. Donovan, Midwest Book Review

*"A compelling story of tenacity, humor and accomplishment."* – Jordan Rich, WBZ CBS Boston

*With New Eyes:*
*The Power of Perspective*

*"Feisty and thought-provoking."* – Midwest Book Review

*"You'll come away looking at the small details in your own life with a little more clarity. For a memoir, there may be no higher praise."* – Self-Publishing Review

*Do your part and help spread the powerful message of Heidi's books by writing online reviews, gifting copies to your clan, and sharing on social media!*

## Here's to looking up!

Printed in Great Britain
by Amazon